PROBLEMS IN ECONOMICS

Dascomb R. Forbush
Clarkson College of Technology

Harper & Row, Publishers
New York   Evanston   San Francisco   London

PROBLEMS IN ECONOMICS

Copyright © 1975 by Harper & Row, Publishers, Inc.

Standard Book Number: 06-042118-5

CONTENTS

ACKNOWLEDGMENTS

To .Peter O. Steiner and Richard G. Lipsey for their innovative interest in having most of these cases and problems published in the *Study Guide* and *Problems* to accompany Lipsey & Steiner *Economics*.

To John Greenman and other members of the Harper & Row editorial staff for making possible the separate publication of this material.

To Dorothy F. Forbush whose hard and skillful work with the more onerous parts of the *Study Guide* allowed me to complete these problems and cases.

To the Clarkson students who provided the audience participation for formulating many of these problems.

INTRODUCTION

This collection of cases and problems is dedicated to the proposition that a good way of understanding economics is to do economics. Doing economics is more than reading a text or listening to lectures. It means studying economic data in order to recognize significant relationships that can help in forecasting the future and in assessing the impact of private and governmental decisions.

You can count on frustrations in working with the problems. Some are quite difficult for introductory students and can be completed only with a running start in class. Some students feel uncomfortable with mathematical manipulations even though nothing more than long-familiar arithmetic and algebra is involved. It is hoped that for most students the satisfactions will outweigh any frustrations. One can really feel that one has mastered a concept when successful in deriving or applying it.

There are 57 problems and cases arranged under 15 headings. The usual arrangement within sections is for the simpler ones to be first and the more complex later. Most courses will use only a substantial fraction of them and will use them in several different ways: as the preassigned basis for class discussion, as written assignments, as background to lectures, as the agenda for mutual solution in class, as previews for possible exam questions, as options for those with particular interests.

While most problems deal with facts of economic life, this book, for better or for worse, has the distinction of having no case studies on the economics of the drug traffic, prostitution, or professional football.

CHANGES IN DEMAND OR SUPPLY

PROBLEM 1

THE IMPACT OF CHANGES IN DEMAND AND SUPPLY

In order to make rough forecasts of the impact of economic changes, fill in the table. Draw new curves on the graphs to aid you. Show the *initial* effects predicted by the hypotheses of the indicated events on the markets. For changes in demand and supply (meaning shifts in the curve), equilibrium price, and quantity, use + or − to show increase or decrease; for no change, use 0. If effect cannot be deducted from the information given, use U.

	Market	Event		D	S	P	Q
1.	Copper wire	Printed circuits are found to be a cheap substitute for wire in radios.		−	0	−	−
2.	Copper wire	The Pentagon greatly increases orders for wire for a new missile system.					
3.	Squid	Other sources of protein become very scarce and expensive, and an MIT group invents a quick way to process squid.					
4.	Petroleum	Incomes and population rise; Arabian oil production and exports are sharply reduced.					

1

5. Cigarettes

A new law requires this notice on each pack: "Warning: The Surgeon-General Has Determined That Cigarette Smoking Is Dangerous to Your Health and May Cause Death from Heart Disease, Lung Cancer, Emphysema and Other Diseases."

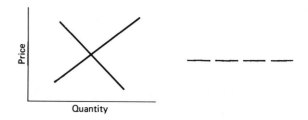

6. Hospital services

Substantially higher wages are paid to hospital employees with no increase in their productivity.

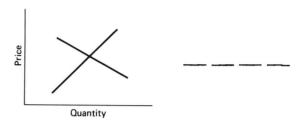

THE CHANGING APPETITES OF AMERICANS

During the period from 1950 to 1972, consumer prices as measured by the Consumer Price Index rose by about 70 percent, and retail food prices increased by a slightly smaller percentage. Per capita disposable income almost tripled, but after adjusting for prices it increased by about 75 percent. The proportion of all consumer expenditures that went for food dropped from about 24 percent to 20 percent.

In the table below of quantities and prices for nine foods, the quantities (Q) are pounds consumed per capita (except for eggs, which are units with the price given for a dozen); the prices (P) are average retail prices (for beef, chuck is used as representative, and for pork, ham). The columns P* list prices divided by the Consumer Price Index (with 1967 = 100, 1950 was .75; 1960, .88; 1969, 1.09; and 1972, 1.24). This can help you to understand whether, in the period covered, a food was becoming cheaper or more expensive relative to all other foods. The ratio of 1972:1950 should help in assessing what changes took place over the entire period.

	Flour			Potatoes			Dried Beans		
	Q	P	P*	Q	P	P*	Q	P	P*
1950	135	9.8	13.2	106	4.6	6.2	8.6	15.3	20.6
1960	118	11.1	12.6	108	7.2	8.2	7.7	16.7	19.0
1969	111	11.6	10.7	115	8.2	7.5	6.5	19.6	18.0
1972	110	11.9	9.6	121	9.3	7.5	6.4	24.8	20.1
1972 ÷ 1950	.8	1.2	.7	1.1	2.0	1.2	.7	1.6	1.0

	Chicken			Beef (Chuck)			Pork (Ham)		
	Q	P	P*	Q	P	P*	Q	P	P*
1950	20.6	59.5	79.9	63.4	60.5	81.2	69.2	60.5	81.2
1960	28.1	42.7	48.5	85.0	61.6	70.0	64.9	60.4	68.6
1969	39.1	42.2	38.7	109.7	70.4	64.6	64.7	72.8	66.9
1972	42.9	41.4	33.5	114.8	82.1	66.5	67.7	78.2	63.3
1972 ÷ 1950	2.1	.7	.4	1.8	1.3	.8	1.0	1.3	.8

	Eggs			Margarine			Butter		
	Q	P	P*	Q	P	P*	Q	P	P*
1950	389	60.4	81.1	6.1	30.8	41.3	10.7	72.9	97.9
1960	335	57.3	65.1	9.4	26.9	30.6	7.5	74.9	85.1
1969	313	62.1	57.0	10.8	27.8	25.5	5.3	84.6	77.7
1972	318	52.4	42.4	11.3	33.1	26.8	5.0	87.1	70.5
1972 ÷ 1950	.8	.9	.5	1.8	1.1	.7	.5	1.2	.7

Questions

1. Which foods fit the hypotheses below and which are apparent exceptions?

	Well Explained by Hypothesis	Apparent Exceptions to Hypothesis
(a) The rise in real income resulted in a greater consumption of high-priced foods.	_____ _____	_____ _____
(b) The rise in real income resulted in a lower consumption of cheaper foods.	_____ _____	_____ _____

(c) A decrease in relative prices (to .7 or below) resulted in increased consumption of the food.

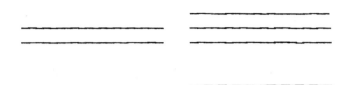

(d) An increase in relative price resulted in reduced consumption of the food.

2. Some changes in dietary preferences that might explain exceptions above follow. List foods whose consumption changes might be explained by each.

    (a) A trend to lighter breakfasts

    (b) Low-carbohydrate diets

    (c) Apprehension about cholesterol or saturated fats

    (d) Emphasis on quick foods (e.g., rise in number of drive-in eating places)

    (e) Changing perception of product through greater familiarity, product improvements, or advertising.

3. The much lower prices for eggs and chickens reflect a change in technology toward a mass-production poultry industry with less feed necessary per egg and per pound of chicken. Show shifts in the supply curves together with the demand changes that would explain the contrasting consumption patterns.

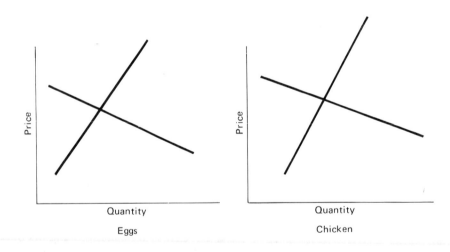

PROBLEM 3

BEEF CONSUMPTION, WITH A TOUCH OF
GRAPHIC AND STATISTICAL ANALYSIS

About 1945, an agricultural economist advanced the following set of hypotheses about beef consumption in the United States:

1. that it varied proportionally with population
2. that it would vary inversely with retail beef prices adjusted to reflect their relationship with the general price level
3. that it would vary directly with fluctuations in real income
4. that it would vary inversely with pork consumption because pork was the closest important substitute

For simplicity, he decided that all of these relationships should be tested as linear and, furthermore, that the explicit use of a population variable could be avoided by placing beef consumption, income, and pork consumption in per capita terms—that is, by dividing each of these variables by population. He collected the information in the table below.

Factors Related to U.S. Beef Consumption, 1922-1941

Observation	Year	Beef Consumption per Capita (Q) (pounds)	Beef Price at Retail Deflated (P)[a] (cents)	Disposable Income per Capita Deflated (Y)[a] (dollars)	Pork Consumption per Capita (C) (pounds)
1	1922	59.1	23.1	452	65.7
2	1923	59.6	23.6	505	74.2
3	1924	59.5	24.1	499	74.0
4	1925	59.5	24.5	507	66.8
5	1926	60.3	24.8	515	64.1
6	1927	54.5	26.5	520	67.7
7	1928	48.7	30.5	533	70.9
8	1929	49.7	32.0	556	69.6
9	1930	48.9	30.3	506	67.0
10	1931	48.6	27.6	474	68.4
11	1932	46.7	25.5	400	70.7
12	1933[b]	51.5	23.3	394	69.6
13	1934[b]	55.9	24.4	430	63.1
14	1935[b]	52.9	31.1	468	48.4
15	1936[b]	58.1	28.9	522	55.1
16	1937	55.2	31.7	537	55.8
17	1938	54.4	28.5	502	58.2
18	1939	54.7	29.7	542	64.7
19	1940	54.9	29.5	575	73.5
20	1941	60.9	30.0	663	68.4
Σ		1,093.6	549.6	10,100	1,315.9
Means		54.7	27.5	505	65.8

[a]Divided by consumer price index, with 1935-1939 = 1.00.
[b]Excludes quantities of beef diverted from normal market channels under emergency government programs.
Source: U.S. Department of Agriculture.

1. Using the symbols in the table for the variables, complete the mathematical function and equation with Q as the independent variable that incorporates the hypotheses above.

$$Q = f(\qquad)$$
$$Q = a - b \underline{\hspace{2cm}} + d \underline{\hspace{2cm}} - g \underline{\hspace{2cm}}$$

Note that these same hypotheses concerning important variables are likely to hold today, except that chicken as well as pork has become a significant substitute for beef. Herbert Hoover used the prospect of "a chicken in every pot on Sunday" as part of the dream of American national prosperity. As late as 1940 only 14 pounds per capita were consumed. In the 1970s, after Minnie Pearl and Colonel Sanders pioneered retail fast-food chains specializing in chicken, over 50 pounds per capita are being consumed.

Chart I

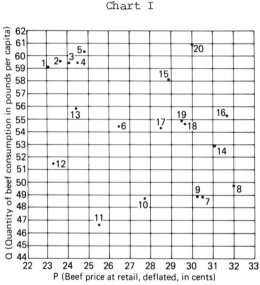

2. The economist constructed the scatter diagram between beef consumption and price, shown as Chart I, and was momentarily discouraged by the results. Looking back at the data, he noticed that low prices seemed to be somewhat associated with low incomes and high prices with high incomes. He decided to indicate low- and high-income years separately by circling dots for the years with incomes less than $475 and placing squares around the years with incomes greater than $530. Do so on Chart I.

3. (a) What kind of price-quantity relationship seems to emerge when years of about the same income are examined? Place light dotted lines between pairs of years such as 1922 and 1931 and 1929 and 1940, when P varied considerably but Y and C were fairly constant.
   (b) Why might you feel justified in ignoring observation 14 (for 1935) in ascertaining this relationship?

4. At this point, he ran a multiple-regression analysis on his data and obtained the following demand function:

$$Q = 90.8 - 1.85P + .083Y - .415C \pm e \quad (e \text{ is an error term})$$

Confirm that this equation corresponds with that set up in question 1. It is apparent that to have a unique relationship of quantity to price, the values of Y and C must be held at a particular level (thus applying the *ceteris paribus* assumption mentioned in the appendix). It is convenient to make them equal to their means: $Y = 505$; $C = 65.8$. This gives, disregarding the error term, $Q = 105.5 - 1.85P$. Fit this line on Chart I.

5. The deviations in the chart from the equation $Q = 105.5 - 1.85P$ are very large. As a matter of fact, using the mean value of beef consumption (54.7) as a predictor yields smaller total deviations. Draw the function $Q = 54.7$ in Chart I to confirm this.

6. (a) It can now be shown graphically that these large deviations reflect the importance of income and pork availability in determining the consumption of beef. In Chart II, the vertical deviations from the line $Q = 105.5 - 1.85P$ in Chart I have been graphed and related to income. What clear relationship does this reveal?

Chart II

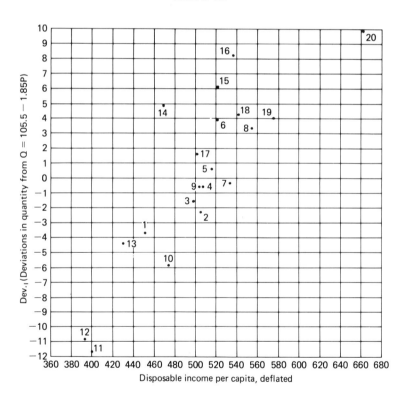

Dev.$_I$ (Deviations in quantity from $Q = 105.5 - 1.85P$)

Disposable income per capita, deflated

(b) Sketch lightly a straight line that you think describes this relationship. As a guide to its slope, it is helpful to connect pairs such as 7 and 11, 10 and 20, and 1 and 18 when pork consumption was about the same. Draw in more decisively the line Dev.$_I$ = .083(Y - 505). Explain briefly the significance of this for predicting beef consumption, remembering that 505 is the mean value of Y.

7. After this allowance for the influence of income on beef consumption in Chart II, the deviations of actual quantity from predicted quantity are much less in Chart II than in Chart I. The worst predictions—that is, largest deviations—are for observations 14-16, years 1935-1937. Why?

8. The vertical deviations from Chart II are graphed on Chart III against pork consumption. Sketch in lightly the straight line that best fits observations. Then draw in the line Dev.$_{II}$ = −.415(C − 65.8). Describe briefly its significance in explaining the deviations in this way, noting that 65.8 is average pork consumption.

Chart III

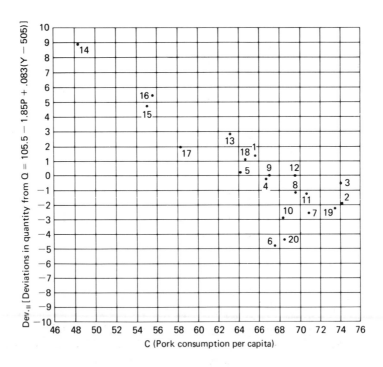

C (Pork consumption per capita)

9. The results from the three graphs can now be combined: the price relationship (Q = 105.5 − 1.85P); the deviations from it explained by income (Dev.$_I$); the remaining deviations explained by pork consumption (Dev.$_{II}$), plus the error term. The equation is: Q = 105.5 − 1.85P + .083(Y − 505) − .415(C − 65.8) ± e. Show that the latter equation reduces to the original demand function derived by multiple-regression methods.

10. Check to see whether this multivariable function did any better than the following simple method of forecast:

$$Q_t = Q_{(t-1)}$$

or, in other words, will this year's beef consumption be the same as last year's? For example, the forecast for 1923 would be 59.1 (the consumption in 1922), and the deviation of the actual 59.6 from this prediction would be +0.5. If the mean beef consumption had been used to estimate the beef consumption in a particular year, we would have had an average deviation of 3.6 pounds a year. This was shown graphically on Chart I. See question 5. Our multivariable equation reduces this average deviation of error term to 1.4 pounds a year.

	Pred.	Dev.		Pred.	Dev.
1 (1922)	_____	_____	11 (1932)	_____	_____
2 (1923)	_____	_____	12 (1933)	_____	_____
3 (1924)	_____	_____	13 (1934)	_____	_____
4 (1925)	_____	_____	14 (1935)	_____	_____
5 (1926)	_____	_____	15 (1936)	_____	_____
6 (1927)	_____	_____	16 (1937)	_____	_____
7 (1928)	_____	_____	17 (1938)	_____	_____
8 (1929)	_____	_____	18 (1939)	_____	_____
9 (1930)	_____	_____	19 (1940)	_____	_____
10 (1931)	_____	_____	20 (1941)	_____	_____

Total deviations _____
Average deviations per year _____
(*Note:* Total and average deviations should ignore sign though you calculate them as actual minus predicted.)

THE ELASTICITY OF DEMAND

PROBLEM 4

RIDERS FOR NIPPON'S MONORAIL

In October, 1968, the Tokyo Monorail Company denied that it was facing bankruptcy. It stated that its operating results were much improved since it had reduced its fare from 250 yen to 150 yen (70 cents to 42 cents) on its 12-mile run from Tokyo airport to the center of the city and by equivalent percentages on shorter commuter runs.

Assume that this price cut was completely responsible for its increase in revenues from 460,000,000 yen in 1966 to 640,000,000 yen in 1967. Calculate the indicated arc elasticity of demand. (*Hint:* As a unit of quantity, use the full-trip equivalent.)

	P	*Q*	Revenue	Elasticity
1966	250	_____	460,000,000	
1967	150	_____	640,000,000	_____

PROBLEM 5

WHAT HAS HAPPENED TO THE RAZOR STROP?

The leading producer of razor strops (whose major use is in sharpening straight razors) compiled these price and sales figures for the industry. Of 11 producers in 1915, only 4 were left by 1949.

Year	Unit Sales	Est. Price
1900	800,000	$1.00
1915	1,750,000	1.50
1930	400,000	1.85
1945	100,000	2.10
1948	80,000	2.10

(a) What, if anything, could you conclude about the price elasticity of demand? Keep in mind the largely agricultural population of the United States in 1900 and King Gillette's patenting of the safety razor shortly before World War I.

(b) Show on the accompanying graph what probably has happened to the demand curve for strops.

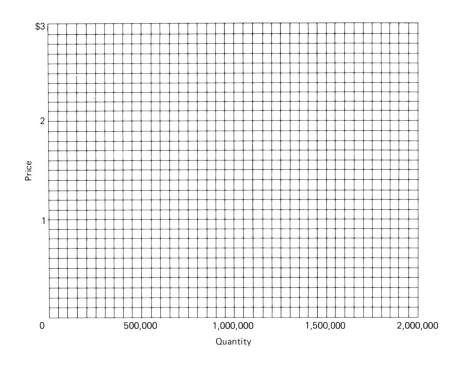

11

PROBLEM 6

RAISING THE RATES ON WATER

In 1969, the trustees of the Village of Potsdam, New York, decided to double the rate charged residents for water, in abundant supply from the local river, in order to pay for their new sewage-treatment plant. Two colleges in the village constitute about half the population when they are in session and pay the same water rate as do households.

Below are listed the Village Administrator's predictions of revenues and the actual results.

Fiscal Year	Price per 1,000 Gallons	Predicted Estimated Revenue	Gallons Sold (thousands)	Actual Revenue
June, 1969-May, 1970	$ .60[a]	$180,000	290,540	$174,325[a]
June, 1970-May, 1971	1.20[a]	360,000	278,045	336,654[a]

[a]Actually the trustees called the extra 60 cents a "sewer tax" and put the extra revenues in the "sewer fund."

Questions

1. What elasticity of demand did the Village Administrator seem to assume here in his prediction for 1970-1971?

2. Compute the approximate elasticity of demand here (round off; two decimal places is close enough).

3. Suppose the trustees decided that this was an easy way to raise money and raised the water rate to $5.00 per 1,000 gallons. Do you think the elasticity would be the same? Why or why not?

4. An alternative method of paying for the sewage-treatment plant would be through increased property taxes. If you were a village trustee, how would you justify doing it instead by, in effect, doubling the price of water?

PROBLEM 7

DEMAND ELASTICITIES FOR BEEF

The demand function for beef given in Problem 3 on beef consumption is
$Q = 90.8 - 1.85P + .083Y - .415C$, where Q is quantity of beef demanded in pounds per capita,
P is the average price per pound in cents (without the decimal point), and Y is disposable
income in dollars per capita (both deflated by the Consumer Price Index, with 1937-1939 prices
taken as 100 percent), and C is pork consumption in pounds per capita.

Questions

1. With Y taken as $500 and C as 65 pounds, this equation becomes $Q = 105.3 - 1.85P$.
Estimate the price elasticity of demand at a price of 25 cents; at a price of 50 cents. (*Hint:*
You may either use the point-elasticity formula recognizing that $\Delta Q/\Delta P$ (or dQ/dP) = -1.85 or
calculate what the percentage change in quantity is for a 1-percent change in price.)

2. Estimate the income elasticity of demand (set P = 25 cents and C = 65 pounds) at an
average income of $500.

Since the time of this beef study, which covered the period 1923-1941, changes have taken
place, but this demand function still does a surprisingly good predicting job. In 1969, the
average price of beef could be estimated at 27 cents (remember this is a *deflated* figure; actually the price was 70.4 cents), approximately the same as the average price from 1923 to
1941. Pork consumption in 1969, approximately 65 pounds per capita, was also almost identical
with the average of forty years ago. Disposable per capita income, however, had risen to almost
$1,200 expressed in 1937-1939 dollars ($3,098 in 1969 dollars).

3. Predict the quantity of beef demanded in 1969 using the demand function above. (Note
that this prediction is close to the actual 1969 figure of 109.7 pounds.)

4. Estimate the price and income elasticities at the 1969 values of the variables.

5. Explain why the calculated price elasticity is less than that you calculated in question 1 and the calculated income elasticity is somewhat greater.

HOUSEHOLD CONSUMPTION BEHAVIOR

_____
_____

PROBLEM 8

MR. AND MRS. INTERMEDIATE BUDGET SMITH AND
THEIR COUSINS CONFRONT INFLATION

The I. B. Smith family as described by the Bureau of Labor Statistics consists of "a 38-year-old employed husband, wife not employed outside of the home (age tactfully not given), an 8-year-old girl, and a 13-year-old boy. It is their consumption patterns that determine the weights used in compiling the Consumer Price Index. The Smiths are an urban family and happen to live in Indianapolis. The residence could just as well have been in Seattle, Portland (Me.), or Cedar Rapids, other cities of average costs. If they moved to Honolulu or Boston, the highest-cost metropolitan areas, the Smiths would need about $2000 more a year to maintain the same standard of living. In Austin, Texas, the lowest-cost metropolitan area for which figures are computed, it could do on $1600 less. Urban but nonmetropolitan living would cost about $1250 less than the $11,446 the Smiths spent. (All figures are based on costs for autumn 1972. You may find later ones in the current _Statistical Abstract of the United States.)_

The I. B. Smiths are at close to the median income for all American families. Actually I. B. has a wage slightly above the median, but since Ms. Smith has not been swept up in the tide of wives with outside work, the total family income is slightly below a median that includes two-income families. The Bureau of Labor Statistics is also interested in cousins of the Smiths: the Lower Budget Johnsons and the Higher Budget Browns, who by remarkable coincidence also have daughters of 8 and sons of 13. Whereas the total cost of living was $11,446 for the Smiths in 1972, it was $7386 for the LBJs and $16,558 for the HBBs. The Johnsons have income greater than that of 30 percent of American families and the Browns income that is less than that of 25 percent of American families. Thus the three families together cover a broad swath of the American middle class.

1972 Budgetary Costs for the Johnsons, Smiths, and Browns						
	Lower Budget		Intermediate Budget		Higher Budget	
	Dollars	Percent	Dollars	Percent	Dollars	Percent
Food	2058	28	2673	23	3370	20
Housing	1554	21	2810	25	4234	26
Clothing and personal care	864	12	1217	11	1770	11
Other consumption	1553	21	2313	20	3088	19
Other costs	365	5	576	5	967	6
Social Security and income taxes	992	13	1857	16	3029	18
Total costs	7386	100	11446	100	16588	100

Questions

1. Which category of consumption expenditure apparently has the lowest income elasticity of demand? Which has the highest? Can you explain these from your experience?

2. From the last quarter of 1972 to the last quarter of 1974 the Consumer Price Index rose from 127 to 154 (1967 = 100). Making the simplified assumption that this increase is applicable for the total costs of each family, what percentage rise in income would be needed to maintain their respective standards of living?

3. During the same period the index for food prices rose from 125 to 168. Which family would have had the most difficult task in adjusting to the inflation, assuming that money income remained constant?

PROBLEM 9

BUDGETING AND PRICE CHANGES, U.S.A.

From 1920 to 1940, consumer prices were generally declining or stable; from 1940 to 1973, consumer prices were occasionally stable but usually rose. This is shown in the table below for food and for all items but food, where prices are expressed in 1957-1959 dollars (i.e., 1957-1959 index = 100). Representative budgets based on the disposable income for an employed family are also shown.

(a) Draw budget lines for 1920, 1940, and 1973 on the graph and complete the table below. Each unit of food and of items other than food is the amount that could be purchased in 1957-1959 for $1. For example, for each $100 of income, 100/.70 or 143 units of food could be bought in 1920.

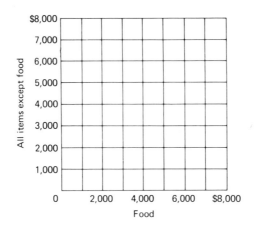

| | Price Indexes | | Family | Food | "Other" |
	Food	"Other"	Income	Intercepts	Intercepts
1920	70	70	$ 2,200		
1940	40	52	2,000		
1973	160	155	11,600		

(b) Does the graph indicate that absolute price declines can be the equivalent of rises in income? Explain briefly.

(c) The budget line for which year is the least steep? _____ Explain.

16

THE CHOICE BETWEEN PRODUCT A AND PRODUCT B

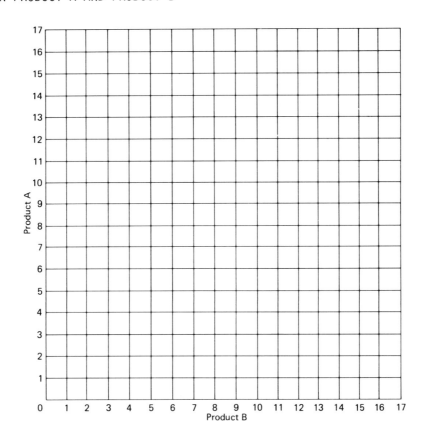

Questions

1. Draw on the figure above the indifference curves for levels of satisfaction indicated by (a) 54, (b) 108, (c) 117, and (d) 144 units in the total utility table that follows. (Note that knowledge of total utilities, while sufficient, is not necessary for indifference analysis.) Label them with letters.

Total Utility from the Consumption of Product A and Product B

Product B

	0	1	2	3	4	5	6	7	8	9	10
0	0	20	38	54	68	80	90	98	104	108	110
1	10	30	48	64	78	90	100	108	114	118	120
2	19	39	57	73	87	99	109	117	123	127	129
3	27	47	65	81	95	107	117	125	131	135	137
4	34	54	72	88	102	114	124	132	138	142	144
5	40	60	78	94	108	120	130	138	144	148	150
6	45	65	83	99	113	125	135	143	149	153	155
7	49	69	87	103	117	129	139	147	153	157	159
8	52	72	90	106	120	132	142	150	156	160	162
9	54	74	92	108	122	134	144	152	158	162	164
10	55	75	93	109	123	135	145	153	159	163	165

(Product A — rows)

Marginal Utility from the Consumption of Product A and Product B

Units of A

or B:	1	2	3	4	5	6	7	8	9	10
MU_A	10	9	8	7	6	5	4	3	2	1
MU_B	20	18	16	14	12	10	8	6	4	2

2. Determine the bundle of goods A and B that maximizes satisfaction for each budget and price combination shown below. Use both the indifference map and the marginal-utility table above to show that the same answer is reached by both approaches, given the approximations necessary.

	Budget	P_A	P_B	Q_A	Q_B	MU_B/MU_A
(a)	$43	$3	$7.00	_____	_____	_____
(b)	43	3	3.50	_____	_____	_____
(c)	15	5	5.00	_____	_____	_____
(d)	40	5	5.00	_____	_____	_____
(e)	45	5	5.00	_____	_____	_____

3. What do you note about the relationship between P_B/P_A and MU_B/MU_A? Is this what the chapter would have led you to expect?

4. What is the relationship between MU_B/MU_A and the marginal rate of substitution expressed as the units of product A that would be substituted for one unit of product B along the indifference curves?

PROBLEM 11

DERIVING HOUSEHOLD DEMAND CURVES FROM INDIFFERENCE MAPS

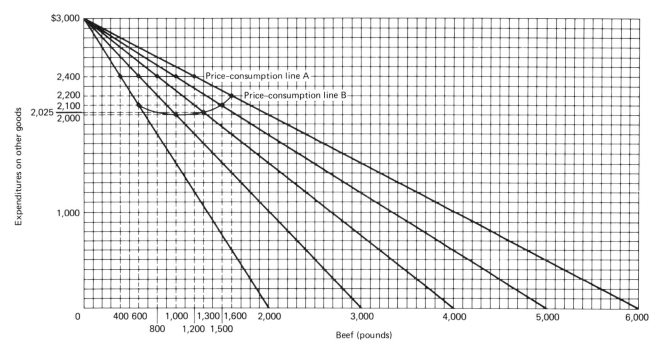

(a) On the graph above, sketch in (using two different colors) indifference maps that could lead to price-consumption lines A and B.

(b) From the price-consumption lines, derive demand curves A and B and enter on the chart below.

P	Q_A	Q_B	Total expenditure on beef A	B
$1.50	——	——	——	——
1.00	——	——	——	——
.75	——	——	——	——
.60	——	——	——	——
.50	——	——	——	——

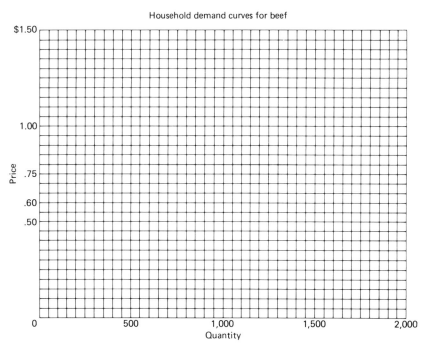

(c) 1. What is price elasticity of demand for household A? _____
    2. At what price does elasticity of demand for household B approach 1? _____

OPPORTUNITY COSTS

PROBLEM 12

THE COST OF VIETNAM, COPPER PENNIES,
AND OTHER GOVERNMENT PROGRAMS

1. (a) Economic arguments against U.S. involvement in the Vietnam war were spelled out in detail before the Democratic National Convention in 1968. The following are two points made by the anti-Administration group whose recommendations were not accepted.

> We [the people] were forced to watch a Congress of the United States . . . cut the budget $6 billion in the last Congress and they cut it out of all the programs affecting the lives of every single American, out of the programs of health, in education and the problems that face our children . . . to meet these problems . . . we will not have the money unless we are able in some fashion to disengage ourselves from the expenditures of our best treasure, our young men, but the fact is that we are spending $30 billion a year in a foreign adventure in Vietnam. It must end. (Ken O'Donnell of Massachusetts)

> We have lost 25,000 young American lives in Vietnam—lives and talents which this nation desperately needs for the solutions of our problems at home. We have spent $100 billion—money and resources which, again, are needed for the repair of the ravages in our own society . . . . (John Gilligan of Ohio)

(b) The U.S. Mint proposed in March, 1974, that the copper penny be replaced with an aluminum cent. One pound of aluminum costing $.29 would make about 500 pennies; 1 pound of copper (plus 5 percent zinc) makes 150 pennies. The Mint was anxious to conserve its copper supply that was needed to produce cupro coins—the nickel-copper sandwiches that replaced silver coinage in 1965.

Rapid increases in copper usage in 1973, combined with little change in world production, resulted in substantial price increases. The London price reached a high of $1.41. While the maximum price under price controls in the United States was $.68, the U.S. government sold copper from its stockpiles at from $1.00 to $1.10 per pound, as American consumption of 2.4 million tons ran ahead of domestic production of 1.8 million tons. With the lifting of price controls the U.S. price could rise to $1.

In the first half of 1974 the Mint was using stockpile copper, which cost the government $.46 a pound in the 1950s. At $1.20 a pound for copper, the cost of making a penny would be greater than 1 cent; at $1.50 the metal alone would be worth more than 1 cent. About 3.6 billion pennies are made each year.

(c) The following statement is from the *Economic Report of the President, 1971:*

> We know that existing programs of Government and probable demands of the private sector could use up all the output we can produce for several years to come. This does

21

not mean that we cannot do anything new. It does mean that we have to choose. If we decide to do something new, or something more, in one direction we will have to give up something elsewhere. There is no unclaimed pool of real resources from which we shall be able to satisfy new demands without sacrificing or modifying some existing claims.

Questions

1. (a) On what basic concept of this chapter did the Convention speakers, the Mint, and the economic report rely?

(b) How is the cost of a government program measured under this concept? Specify.

(c) What is the cost to the U.S. economy of using copper instead of aluminum pennies? Be as specific as possible.

2. (a) Draw up a production-possibility boundary for production for civilian and for military use by the economy. On it indicate the decision the anti-Administration convention delegates advocated. *(Note:* Assume that military production was about one-eighth of the total output and Vietnam expenditures were about one-third of the military budget.)

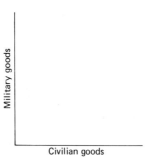

(b) In part (a) above, what assumptions did you make about the employment of resources and the efficiency with which they were used?

(c) Have events since August, 1968, indicated that their arguments about a preferable allocation of productive resources have been accepted?

PROBLEM 13

DIAMOND'S FOR RENT

In the late 1960s, B. G. Diamond changed the location of his jewelry store to a newly developed suburban shopping area, where he built a new store in a corner location for $100,000. His operations were successful there, and his stated profits increased substantially. Diamond's 1973 statement follows:

Gross margin (sales—cost of goods sold)		$75,000
Wages and salaries (including $15,000 salary for himself)	$35,000	
Taxes, depreciation, and insurance on store	7,000	
Interest paid on bank loans of $50,000 @ 8%	4,000	
Other expenses	6,000	52,000
		$23,000

In early 1974, one of the rapidly growing national jewelry chains offered Diamond $2,000 a month rent on his store under a long-term lease (Diamond would have to meet the expense items: taxes, insurance, and depreciation) and an opportunity to sell out his inventory and fixtures for $80,000. He could retire his bank loan and invest the other $30,000 at 8 percent and take a standing offer of $20,000 to join a downtown department store as manager of its jewelry department.

B. G. Diamond estimated that his store's future results would be similar to those in 1973, because, although business had been increasing, the national chain was likely to locate somewhere in the area and its competition would reduce future gains.

Revise his income statement to estimate economic profits and predict his decision.

PROBLEM 14

PROJECT VOLUNTEER: THE COSTS OF
AN ALL-VOLUNTEER ARMED FORCE

The authority to draft men for the armed forces expired July 1, 1973, after 33 years of almost uninterrupted dependence on conscription and 6 months of no draft calls. A first step in this change of public policy was the Gates Commission report, which is extensively quoted below. The second step was a pay raise in 1971 to bring salaries up to civilian standards for recruits and junior officers. (No significant increase had taken place since 1952, and the $326 monthly pay for a recruit authorized in 1973 far exceeded the $134 of 1971. Both figures are exclusive of living expenses.) The third step was to pull troops out of Vietnam.

In March, 1969, President Nixon appointed an Advisory Committee on an All-Volunteer Armed Force under the chairmanship of Thomas S. Gates, Jr., former secretary of defense. Its charge was to develop a "comprehensive plan for eliminating conscription" and to "study the estimated costs and savings resulting from an all-volunteer force."*

In February, 1970, the Commission, which included economists Milton Friedman and Alan Greenspan, along with college presidents, a student, retired generals, and business leaders, submitted its report.

Its recommendations, in brief, were as follows:

We unanimously believe that the nation's interests will be better served by an all-volunteer force, supported by an effective standby draft, than by a mixed force of volunteers and conscripts; that steps should be taken promptly to move in this direction; and that the first indispensable step is to remove the present inequity in the pay of men serving their first term in the armed forces. The United States has relied throughout its history on a voluntary armed force except during major wars and since 1948. A return to an all-volunteer force will strengthen our freedoms, remove an inequity now imposed on the expression of the patriotism that has never been lacking among our youth, promote the efficiency of the armed forces, and enhance their dignity. It is the system for maintaining standing forces that minimizes government interference with the freedom of the individual to determine his own life in accord with his values.

The Commission stressed the fact that despite an increased budget, the costs would be lower:

Although the *budgetary expense* of a volunteer armed force will be higher than for the present mixed force of volunteers and conscripts, the *actual cost* will be lower. This seemingly paradoxical statement is true because many of the costs of manning our armed forces today are hidden and are not reflected in the budget. Men who are forced to serve in the military at artificially low pay are actually paying a form of tax which subsidizes those in the society who do not serve. Furthermore, the output of the civilian economy is reduced because more men serve in the military than would be required for an all-volunteer force of the same strength. This cost does not show up in the budget. Neither does the loss in output resulting from the disruption in the lives of young men who do not serve. Neither do the costs borne by those men who do not serve, but who rearrange their lives in response to the possibility of being drafted. Taking these hidden and neglected costs into account, the actual cost to the nation of an all-volunteer force will be lower than the cost of the present force.

The report continues: "When the hidden costs of conscription are fully recognized, the cost of an all-volunteer armed force is unquestionably less than the cost of a force of equal

*Quotations in this problem are from *The Volunteer Army: Report of the Gates Commission* (USGPO, 1970).

size and quality manned wholly or partly through conscription."

All-volunteer costs are lower for four reasons. First, both budget expenditures and real costs will be reduced by lowering the turnover rate. Inductees generally do not reenlist, volunteers frequently do; and the terms of voluntary enlistments are three to four years, not the two years under the draft. The Commission estimates the reduction in training costs for the equivalent of a 2.5 million army will amount to $675 million a year. Fewer training personnel means that only 2,440,000 can do the job of 2,500,000 men at a cost reduction of another $68 million a year.

Second, "conscription induces the military services to use men inefficiently." They fail to mechanize, to minimize maintenance costs on equipment, and to substitute civilians where appropriate because they are misled by the apparent low cost of conscripted manpower. The report anticipates a saving of $100 million by the appropriate substitution of civilians alone.

Third, "conscription, whether by lottery or on a selective basis, is relatively insensitive to the alternative value of the draftee in the civilian economy and to his tastes for military employment." This cost is an estimated $2 billion tax on draftees and draft-induced volunteers, as described below. But both the hidden tax and the budget expenditures needed could be reduced by eliminating situations similar to the following: A draftee who would volunteer only if compensation were $8,000 is replaced by a true volunteer at $6,000. Whether the $2,000 represents a difference based on civilian productivity or a difference in taste for military life, it is a true cost under the draft.

"Finally there are many subtle costs imposed by conscription that are no less real for their subtlety. Their effects rarefy throughout society." Such costs include those to:

1. the potential draftee—an erosion of the ideals of patriotism and service, a distortion of career plans toward seeking exemptions, a propensity to earlier marriage, the risks of five-year prison terms for those lost in an intricate legal maze
2. the military—lottery selection compels some to serve with "no taste or talent for military life"; these men create morale and disciplinary problems
3. schools and colleges—the presence of "young men more interested in exemptions than education adds to the forces of disruption on the campus, imposing costs on all members of a university community"

The Commission stated that indirect evidence (which was not spelled out) suggests that these costs *may* be 1.5 times the implicit tax, or about $3 billion.

The report went on to clarify the nature of conscription as a tax:

Under conscription, each inductee and reluctant volunteer is compelled to render services to the government. He is required to pay a tax—a tax paid (and collected) in kind rather than cash—but the form of the payment does not alter the substance of the relationship. The amount of the tax is the difference between the pay that the inductee or reluctant volunteer actually receives as a first-term serviceman and the pay that would be required to induce him to enlist. Even true volunteers who serve in a mixed force are paid less than they would receive in a volunteer force. In that sense, they too are taxed by conscription.

Prevailing government accounting practices do not recognize taxes paid in kind. Therefore, the tax on the first-term servicemen never gets recorded in the budget either as revenue or as expenditure. In an all-volunteer force, the additional military compensation will be paid in cash or other benefits, and the taxes to make those payments will be collected in cash. Recorded budget expenditures will have to be increased to reflect these payments. This is the source of the budget "increase" we have estimated for an all-volunteer force . . . . What appears on the surface to be an increase in expenditures is actually a shift in the tax burden from first-term servicemen to taxpayers at large . . . . This shift in tax burden lies at the heart of resistance on "cost" grounds to an all-volunteer armed force. Indeed, this shift in tax burden explains how conscription gets enacted in the first place. In a political democracy conscription offers the general public an opportunity to impose a disproportionate share of defense costs on a minority of the population.

The size of this tax was estimated as $2 billion: $1.5 billion represented the difference between the potential civilian earnings and the military earnings of draftees and draft-induced volunteers; $500 million, the additional compensation necessary to induce the same individuals to become true volunteers. The $2 billion amounted to 48 percent of the income draftees and draft-induced enlistees could have earned in civilian life. This rate of implicit taxation, it was noted, is triple that for others with similar potential earnings who pay about 15 percent in income taxes—a discrimination against a small minority that the Commission challenged as being of "questionable morality," particularly because it falls on individuals whose income was low.

In addition to replacing this tax in kind, the Commission estimated that explicit budget expenditures would have to include an estimated $1.25 billion (calculated at pre-Vietnam levels) to reflect the fact that under a voluntary army many soldiers would be paid more than their acceptable minimum to get them to enlist (note the rising supply curve in the diagrams in the text chapter).

In the February 28, 1974, issue of *Commanders Digest* (Department of Defense), William K. Brehm, Assistant Secretary of Defense for Manpower, made a special status report on the all-volunteer forces. He sought to answer four questions that remained questions of controversy: whether enough recruits are being obtained; whether quality standards were being achieved; whether there was significant racial imbalance; and whether costs were too high.

Concerning quantity, he reported that the actual recruitments were at 93 percent of

target, which was 419,000 for fiscal 1974, and that true volunteers were running 60 percent above the 253,000 in fiscal year 1971, when a majority of 549,000 recruits were drafted or draft-motivated. The greatest difficulty in recruiting was apparently in the combat arms even with an additional enlistment bonus of $2500.

On the criterion of a high-school diploma, there was a modest drop-off with the new enlistments showing the following percentages: Army, 54%; Navy, 72%; Marines, 51%; and Air Force, 95%. The Army had been 67% in 1964 and all services 68% in 1964 and 1973. The emphasis on high-school equivalency work in service had slightly increased the Army's enlisted high-school graduates from 1971 to 1972.

The question of racial balance has brought expressions of concern from a wide spectrum of views, from the militant to the reactionary. Charles B. Rangel, a black congressman from New York, predicted that "America's oppressed races would be fighting and dying so that the affluent whites can continue to enjoy the fruits of imperialism." On the reactionary side, the inducement of middle-class wages for poor blacks is seen to produce potential dangers of a militarily trained minority. In early 1974 the black percentages ranged from 8% in the Navy to 14% in the Air Force, 18% in the Marines, and 20% in the Army. The Department ot Defense takes the position, "As an equal opportunity employer, performance is the sole basis for accepting or excluding any individual."

Brehm found that the only costs that should be charged to the all-volunteer force for the fiscal year 1974 are $733,600,000 to cover recruitment sales efforts, advertising, bonuses and scholarships, and improvements to base services, and that these are largely offset by the benefits of reduced turnover.

The average productive time after training per recruit has been increased from 21 months to 33 months in the combat army. This will save $100,000,000 a year in training costs and produce more experience and readiness. From 1967 to 1969 the average service per enlisted accession produced 3.3 productive man-years; it now is up to 4.1 years and will increase to 4.5 years after 1975. The annual savings will be over $500,000,000 by 1976.

The big budget item in the volunteer army, originally called Project Volunteer, was the $3 billion appropriated to raise first-termer salaries and to improve working conditions (better quarters, no K.P.). In early 1971 the first-termer earned less than 60 percent of what his nonmilitary friends could earn. This item was not counted as a cost by Brehm.

> Our first-termers—many of them draftees—were bearing far more than their share of the cost of the Nation's defense program. They were being heavily taxed through the imposition of poverty level wages . . . . The situation was disgraceful for a country as rich as ours. But more to the point, one who contemplates a return to the draft should not count on rolling back the wages of the first-termer to reduce personnel costs. It simply will not happen.

Questions

1. How can higher government budget expenditures for an all-volunteer army be compatible with lower actual costs?

2. Draw a supply curve for military personnel that recognizes the variation in preferences for military services and in employment alternatives among Americans?

3. Show on this diagram the areas corresponding to the addition to the budget estimated to be necessary to remove the tax in kind on draftees and draft-induced volunteers. Also show the estimated amount to be paid to the true volunteers and others beyond the level of this "tax." (This can be done only approximately because, under our mixed lottery-exemption draft, soldiers have come from many places on the supply curve.)

4. Why does the additional budgetary cost of an all-volunteer army increase more rapidly than the size of the army needed?

5. Do you think the question of racial balance relevant for the armed forces? If so, what measures would you take?

6. In early 1975, when the last draftee was discharged, all service quotas were being fully met with substantial waiting lists for preferred branches. The unemployment rate had risen from 5.2 percent in February 1974 to 8.2 percent in February 1975. Is there a probable relationship between these two developments? Explain.

7. Which of these appeals used by the Army would you expect to be most effective in recruiting?

    You start at $306 per month and may not have to spend it.
    Live and work in places tourists only visit.
    Go to college in the Army or after.
    The job you learn in the Army is yours to keep.

PRODUCTION FUNCTIONS AND COST CURVES

PROBLEM 15

THE CASE OF THE ECONOMICALLY EFFICIENT CHINESE AIRSTRIP

The name of this case comes from the building of airstrips in China during World War II, using extremely primitive methods, with baskets, shovels, and other hand tools. The following table outlines the factor requirements for three productions methods for an airstrip: the manual method (A); a semicapitalistic method using trucks and bulldozers (B); and a highly sophisticated method involving heavy earth-movers, pavers, and other machinery (C). The factors used are designated as M (capital—machinery), T (capital—simple tools), U (unskilled labor), and S (skilled labor). Capital is measured in arbitrary units which take time into account; labor is measured in man-days. Units of factors required are given in the columns headed "Req." Prices are given for three types of economy: the underdeveloped economy under war conditions, the developing nation, and the industrialized nation. Your job is to uncover the economically efficient method for each economy.
(a) Fill in the worksheet below.

Cost Analysis Worksheet

Factor	Price of Factor	Method A Req.	Method A TC	Method B Req.	Method B TC	Method C Req.	Method C TC
Underde-veloped (war)							
M	$5,000	0	0	20		100	
T	5	2,000	10,000	500		200	
U	1	100,000	100,000	20,000		2,000	
S	50	0	0	200		1,000	
Total Cost			$110,000				

Factor	Price of Factor	Method A Req.	Method A TC	Method B Req.	Method B TC	Method C Req.	Method C TC
Developing nation							
M	$ 300	0		50		100	
T	5	2,000		500		200	
U	1	100,000		20,000		2,000	
S	15	0		200		1,000	
Total Cost							

Cost Analysis Worksheet (continued)

Industrial nation		Req.	TC	Req.	TC	Req.	TC
M	$ 100	0	_____	20	_____	100	_____
T	5	2,000	_____	500	_____	200	_____
U	25	100,000	_____	20,000	_____	2,000	_____
S	50	0	_____	200	_____	1,000	_____
Total Cost							

(b) By filling in the worksheet, you can ascertain the economically efficient method for each economy: underdeveloped (war) _____; developing nation _____; industrial nation _____.

30

PROBLEM 16

THE RISING COST OF DRIVING AN AUTOMOBILE

A.   On June 13, 1971, the *New York Times* reported that the American Automobile Association's "cost-of-driving index" had risen to $1,550, an increase of $102 over the 1969 level. The $1,550 assumed 10,000 miles driven (the national average), made the calculations for full-sized Chevrolets (Impalas) with automatic transmission and power steering, and based the depreciation on a trade-in after four years.

The average costs were as follows:

	Average per mile (cents)	
Variable Costs	1971	1969
Gas and oil	2.96	2.76
Maintenance	.73	.68
Tires	.56	.51
Total per mile	4.25	3.95
	Annually (dollars)	
Fixed Costs		
Fire and theft insurance	$ 62	$ 44
Collision insurance	125	102
Liability insurance	175	154
License and registration	25	24
Depreciation	738	729
Total per year	$1,125	$1,053

Questions

1. Assuming that the total variable costs vary proportionally with output (this means that AVC = MC; why?), complete this cost output table for 1971.

Output in Miles	TFC (dollars)	TVC	TTC	AFC	AVC = MC (cents)	ATC
5,000	$1,125				4.25	
10,000	$1,125				4.25	
15,000	$1,125				4.25	

2. Is it fair that firms were paying their employees 11 cents per mile for travel expenditures in view of the average cost of driving?

3. Is depreciation necessarily a fixed cost? (If 60,000 miles are driven before the end of four years, the agency making the estimates would use the four-year trade-in value.)

4. What economic costs have been omitted from the above analysis?

B. Runzheimer and Company, the source of the *New York Times* figures, computed costs for different types of cars in the Chicago area, where both fixed costs (higher insurance) and operating costs (more stop-and-go driving) were higher.

	Gas, Oil Costs (cents per mile)	Other Variable Costs (cents per mile)	Annual Fixed Costs (dollars)
Full-sized Chevrolet	3.00	1.45	$1,385
American compact	2.40	1.25	1,130
Volkswagen	1.50	1.10	838

Questions

1. What are the per-mile costs for 10,000 miles per year for each car?

2. According to the text, a profit-maximizing firm will choose the lowest long-run cost curve for achieving a particular output. Why do not all firms operate fleets of Volkswagens?

3. In late 1973 and early 1974 gasoline and oil prices jumped by almost 50 percent. How would this change the per-mile costs shown above? How would it change the cost advantage that the Volkswagen and American compact have over a full-sized Chevrolet?

PROBLEM 17

SUPERMAMMOTH SUPERTANKERS?

The largest supertanker operating at the start of 1969 was the *Universe Iran* rated at 326,933 deadweight ton-carrying capacity, a few hundred tons more than 4 sister ships of the same design. This was over 14 times as large as the largest tanker of 1945, but the end may not yet be in sight. Even in 1967, *Fortune* noted negotiations for a 500,000-ton tanker and quoted an American expert as seeing "no objection or technical diffitulty in the way of the one-million-ton tanker." And these are long tons of 2,240 pounds of deadweight capacity.

On May 1, 1973, the largest registered tanker was the *Globtik Tokyo* of 438,664 deadweight tons. Its length of 1,234 feet exceeded that of the Universe group by 105 feet; its beam of 203 feet was 24 feet greater. (Consult "Lloyd's Registry of Ships" figures in the *World Almanac* for possible new leaders.)

This table summarizes the data from 1945 to 1973:

	Number of Tankers Registered	Deadweight Capacity (tons)	Supertanker Size (tons)	Tanker Mean Size (tons)
1945	1,911	24,000,000	23,000	12,500
1956	2,778	45,000,000	45,000	16,000
1966	3,524	103,000,000	210,000	29,000
1969	4,071	133,500,000	325,000	33,000
1973	4,581	193,000,000	438,000	42,000

What are the advantages of large tankers? As listed in *Fortune* in September, 1967, they include:

1. The size and expense of the instrument-packed and expensive deck-house remain largely unchanged as the size of the tanker increases.
2. Frequent repetition of steel shapes for cargo tanks allows mass-production techniques
3. Steel thickness in big ships does not increase with size of vessel, partly because the danger of sitting on the top of a single wave with consequent strain to midsection is reduced.
4. Longer ships do not require proportionally more power to move through water, so increases in engine size are far less than proportional.
5. In the highly automated, low-cost shipyards of Japan these considerations add up to a cost of $200 per deadweight ton for a 25,000-ton vessel, $104 for a 50,000-tonner, and $75 for tankers of 150,000 tons and up.
6. Large tankers are much more economical to operate. The 30-man crew of an automated 150,000-ton tanker is the same size as that of an older 25,000-ton tanker and, as suggested above, the fuel-cost increases are less than proportional.

Is the limit in sight?

At least temporarily, available handling facilities impose a limit on ship size. Few docks can accommodate 200,000-ton ships for unloading or for overhaul; in 1967, no U.S. port could handle anything over 100,000 tons.

The Suez Canal could handle only 80,000-ton ships full and 200,000-ton ships empty (its closing in 1956 set off the size explosion). One oil executive has stated that "the 300,000-tonners are too inflexible; you have to dredge oceans for them." Many harbors and even such ocean channels as the Malacca Straits are too shallow.

Unanticipated large technical risks developed. Three supertankers, including the 207,000-ton *Maripassa,* had explosions during tank cleaning. The *Maripassa* sank (fortunately, it carried no oil). Other large tankers buckled at launching. Such difficulties have raised annual insurance costs to over $1,000,000 a ship, four times anticipated costs, according to *Environment* magazine (March, 1971).

The largest tanker spill yet, from the *Torrey Canyon* (118,000 tons), involved environmental and esthetic damage of such extent that commercial insurance companies have declined to offer oil-disaster insurance, forcing tanker operators to establish their own insurance pools. But even an accidental spill as large as that of the cargo of a very large tanker would be a small fraction of the 5 to 10 million tons of petroleum man deposits in the oceans each year.

Only three ports in the United States have channels deep enough to handle mammoth tankers (in 1971, 133 were of between 200,000 and 325,000 tons' capacity): Long Beach, California; Machiasport, Maine; and Seattle, Washintgon; and none of these has dock facilities. A setback to American use of supertankers was the rejection, in June, 1971, of a plan for a superport six miles off the Delaware shore in Chesapeake Bay. A commission recommended that "there be no further intrusion of incompatible heavy industry into Delaware's coastal zone since pollution and other adverse environmental and social effects . . . present serious threats to the coastal environment, the natural resources of the bays and the quality of life in Delaware *(Wall Street Journal,* June 30, 1971).

Questions

1. To what economic demand and supply developments does the technological development of supertankers seem to have been a response?

2. (a) Supertankers seem to be a clear illustration of what kind of economies?

   (b) What evidence is cited that both labor and capital productivity have been increased with the size of the tanker?

3. From the first table it is apparent that many small tankers are still operating; why may they still be able to compete?

4. Unresolved in early 1975 is whether the United States should have deepwater port facilities to handle supertankers. These could be in a harbor such as Machiasport but more likely would use offshore mooring buoys with pipelines discharging to shore. Cite arguments for and against this development.

PROBLEM 18

FROM PRODUCTION FUNCTION TO COST CURVES

This problem requires you to generate basic relationships from the following single line of information which contains a two-factor function and prices of the factors:

$$Q = 10L^{2/3}C^{1/3} \qquad\qquad P_L = P_C = \$3$$

where Q = units of output, L = units of labor, C = units of capital, and P_L and P_C = the prices of labor and capital, respectively.

You will find it of great value to think through the economic significance of each step.

Questions

1. On the graph below, draw the isoquants for 100, 200, and 300 units of output. Inputs have been computed from the cubed version of the production function, that is $Q^3/1,000 = L^2C$. The isoquant for 158.74 has been drawn in. The significance of this unusual quantity will become apparent later.

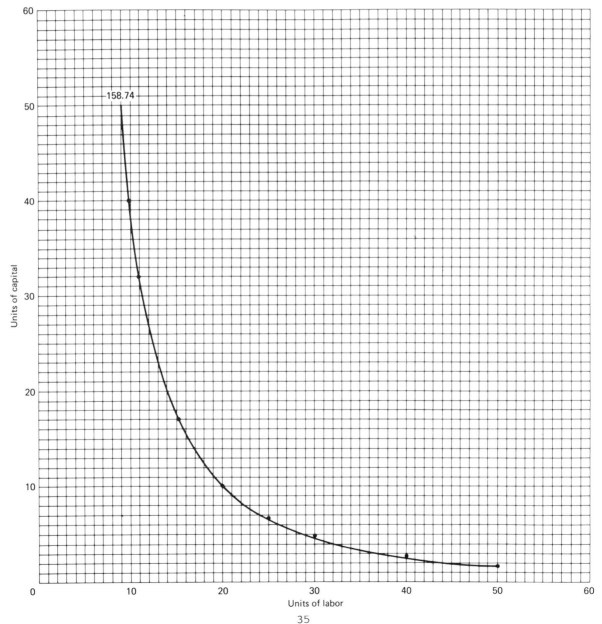

35

Isoquant 100		Isoquant 158.74		Isoquant 200		Isoquant 300	
L	C	L	C	L	C	L	C
4.1	60.0	8.9	50.0	11.5	60.0	21.2	60.0
5.0	40.0	10.0	40.0	15.0	35.6	25.0	43.2
7.1	20.0	15.0	17.7	20.0	20.0	30.0	30.0
10.0	10.0	20.0	10.0	28.3	10.0	40.0	16.9
15.0	4.4	25.0	6.4	40.0	5.0	52.0	10.0
30.0	1.1	30.0	4.4	50.0	3.2	60.0	7.5
60.0	0.3	40.0	2.5	60.0	2.2		
		50.0	1.6				

2. Determine graphically the lowest-cost method of producing 200 units assuming momentarily that P_L = \$3 and P_C = \$1. (You will want the isocost line with a slope of -3 that is tangent to the 200 isoquant. Why?) Enter the production method below as indicated by the combination of factors and check with the total cost given.

L = _____ ; C = _____ ; TC = ___\$78.30___

3. Now take the initial value of P_L and P_C = \$3 and determine the minimum cost methods of producing 100, 200, and 300 units; enter the missing answers in the table below. (You may differ slightly with the answers given.)

Q	L (units)	C (units)	TC (dollars)
0	0	0	0
100.00	_____	_____	56.70
158.74	20.0	10.0	90.00
200.00	25.2		
300.00	_____	18.9	_____

4. Comparing 2 and 3 above, note that, as a result of the rise in P_C from \$1 to \$3, total costs of producing 200 units have risen by _____, and _____ units of L have been substituted for _____ units of C in the best production method for an output of 200.

5. Now assume that capital is fixed at 10 units. This makes it a _____ -run problem rather than a _____ -run problem as in part 3. Show graphically what combinations of factors are optimal for outputs of 100, 200, and 300, and fill in the table below.

Q	L (units)	C (units)	TC (dollars)
0	0	10	_____
100.00	_____	10	
158.74	20	10	90.0
200.00	_____	10	_____
300.00	_____	10	_____

6. (a) Estimate the marginal productivities and compute the average productivities of labor from the data in part 5.

Output	L		MP$_L$	AP$_L$
0				
100.00	_____	>	_____	_____
158.74	20	>	_____	7.94
200.00	_____	>	_____	_____
300.00	_____	>	_____	_____

36

(b) Are the data in this problem consistent with the hypothesis of eventually diminishing marginal and average returns?

7. The tables in parts 5 and 3 now permit us to calculate both the short- and long-run cost curves. Fill in the following table.

Q	Short-run Costs (5)							Long-run Costs (3)		
	TC	TFC	TVC	MC	AFC	AVC	AC	TC	AC	MC
0	——	——	——	>	——	——	——	0		>
100.00	——	——	——	> .517	——	——	——	56.70	.567	> .567
158.74	90.0	30	60.0	> .603	.189	.378	.567	90.00	.567	> .567
200.00	114.9	30	84.9	>	——	——	——	——	——	>
300.00	——	——	——		——	——	——	——	——	

8. Graph the average and marginal cost curves below (long run and short run).

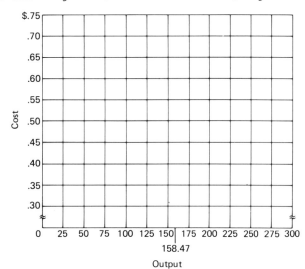

9. Where is the common point of the SRAC and the LRAC? _____ What is the capacity (as defined in Chapter 11) of a plant with 10 units of capital? _____
This firm faces (decreasing/constant/increasing) returns to scale.

PROBLEMS OF GROWTH AND SOCIAL COSTS

PROBLEM 19

THE END OF THE SST?

Three administrations struggled with the question of what role the U.S. government should play in the development of a supersonic transport airplane. In the spring of 1971, after $1 billion had been spent, the Senate finally terminated the government subsidy. Conflicting technological, nationalistic, economic, and environmental values were involved. The major U.S. commitment to the SST occurred after Pan-American Airways announced in mid-1963 that it planned to purchase six Concordes, the Anglo-French supersonic transport. President Kennedy, in announcing a design competition for an American model, stated, "An SST is essential to a strong and forward-looking nation."

In 1967, after the Boeing Company had won the design competition, which was financed 75 percent by the government and 25 percent by the companies involved, a major controversy developed when Boeing and General Electric, which would furnish the engines, insisted that the government finance 90 percent of the design and prototype building stages. In the words of *Fortune* (February, 1970):

> The plan to build an American supersonic transport promises one of the most remarkable advances of our time: An airplane carrying some 350 passengers for 4,000 miles at 1,800 mph. . . . For all its promise, however, this great national undertaking has been so repeatedly delayed by doubting officials and politicians, design problems, and financing difficulties, that the U.S. is being dragged into the supersonic era like a limp student demonstrator protesting the draft.

Fortune itself provided part of the explanation in its estimates that the SST at best would be far less profitable than the Boeing 747, which was nearing the production phase. The government finally went along with the 90 percent share, which, however, was to be repaid plus 6 percent interest from royalties on the sales of the plane—a rather meagre rate of return, considering the great risks and the 10 to 15 percent average return prevailing in U.S. industry.

In 1969, after considerable procrastination, the Nixon Administration supported continued financing. The public was given some semi-assurances that the SST would not be allowed to fly supersonically over "populated areas," which in some versions became the "continental United States," because of the sonic booms.

The critical vote in March, 1971, involved only an additional $79,000,000 appropriation for fiscal 1971, but implied an additional $400,000,000 commitment for the building of two prototypes by 1973. The government had already advanced $864,000,000 for development. In addition, there was serious question about the future availability of perhaps $3,000,000,000 of private capital for financing commercial production after the building of the prototypes.

The technological argument presented by Boeing stressed productivity: "Trip time from New York to London will be reduced from about 7 hours to only 2-3/4 hours . . . the SST will be almost twice as productive as the 747 in terms of seat miles per hour." This increased productivity was shown on the time chart reproduced below. It went on to suggest possible externalities: ". . . in particular the development of titanium technology will benefit future U.S. subsonic jet programs . . . other industries may well benefit."

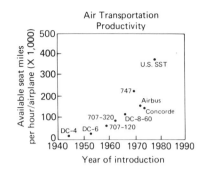

Source: "The United States Supersonic Transport," Boeing Company, Commercial Airplane Group, Supersonic Transport Division.

The nationalist argument had probably been strengthened by the fact that prototype models of the Anglo-French Concorde and the Soviet TU-144 were flying. Despite the view of most economists that balance-of-payments arguments were irrelevant (over the long run, our international payments will roughly balance in any case), Boeing stressed potential net export business of $10 billion and the avoidance of imports of $12 billion between 1975 and 1990.

Concerns about the environment were only partly met by assurances that only over-water flights would be made. Representative Yates, for example, predicted the "inevitability of efforts to remove the supersonic ban over land." More advanced sound suppressors than any available would be needed to meet the new lower standards for airport noise. Although air pollutants per passenger mile would be negligible compared with the emissions of automobiles, they would be double those of subsonic jets. Particular concern was expressed about the unknown effects on weather and on the ozone layer of introducing carbon dioxide and water vapor into the stable air mass of the stratosphere.

The short-run economic argument for the SST had been strengthened by the recession of 1970-1971 and by the particularly high unemployment among aerospace professionals and workers (partly associated with cutbacks in space programs and defense procurement). However, the near cessation of growth in international air travel threw great doubt on long-run demand projections using the 10 percent annual growth rate referred to by the plane's proponents.

There was virtual unanimity among economists who differed on other issues that government should cease its support for the SST. In comments invited by Senators Fulbright and Proxmire, they stressed market-test and opportunity-cost arguments:

If the SST is worth building, the market will make it in Boeing's interest to build it without a subsidy; if a subsidy is needed, the SST should not be built. (Professor Milton Friedman, University of Chicago)

We ought to insist that Congressmen be just as tough-minded with our tax dollars as investors are with their own. If such a standard prevailed, there would be no need for lobbying; SST advocates could make their case to the investors. If the case were a convincing one, the money would be forthcoming. If it were not, the SST would not be built. This is a free enterprise rule that is applied to other marvels of modern technology from new computers to new chemical processes. I find no reason why SST should be made an exception. (Professor Merton Peck, Yale University)

The development and construction of these super planes—as their proponents rightly claim—will absorb many billions of dollars of public and private—but mostly public— money, several hundred thousand years of skilled labor and huge amounts of other valuable economic resources. At a time when the shortage of such resources compels us to forgo badly needed improvements in public health care, education, housing, and mass transportation, to give priority to the SST is nothing short of frivolous. (Professor Wassily Leontief, Harvard University)

Henry Wallich (Professor of Economics, Yale University), the one dissenter in the testimony, said that we must proceed on the assumption that subsidized "supersonic transports will fly, ours or someone else's. . . . Failure to build could inflict lasting balance of payments damage with little compensating environmental gain." (The above quotations are from the *Congressional Record,* September 17, 1970.)

No private financing was available when the government withdrew its support. Estimates of initial operating costs per seat mile (crew, insurance, fuel, and depreciation) that were 60 percent higher than those for the Boeing 747 and the possibility of subsidized foreign competition probably contributed to the lack of private financial enthusiasm. Boeing's arguments for combined government participation were at least for the time rejected:

1. The SST program is more than a commercial venture for the manufacturers and the airline; it relates to our nation's technical and economic leadership and a basic national resource—transportation.
2. Commercial supersonic flight is inevitable. The government has the opportunity to "prime the pump" and hasten a new transportation plateau.

In 1974 the Russians were reported to be in substantial production of the TU-144 for their internal use. There were only six firm orders for the Concorde (from the state-owned airlines of France and Great Britain). The high initial cost of about $60,000,000, plus high fuel costs and low passenger capacity (125) indicated the necessity for government subsidies. Abandonment of the Concorde seemed possible.

Questions

1. What might explain the lack of enthusiasm of private financial markets for a plane that was predicted to be "twice as productive" as the successful Boeing 747?

2. Are you satisfied with leaving the provision of SST services to the test of a free market? If so, how do you distinguish this case from that of college education, space exploration, national parks?

3. If Russia, France, and England subsidize the commercial production and perhaps operation of their smaller, slower SSTs, as seems very possible, would your position be one or more of the following?
    (a) The government should act to revive the U.S. SST program.
    *(b) The United States should restrict use of the Concorde and TU-144 by forbidding landing in this country.
    (c) American carriers should be compensated for loss of revenue to subsidized lines and given operating subsidies if neccesary to run imported SSTs profitably.
    *(d) The United States should subsidize the sale abroad of such subsonics as the Boeing 747 to help maintain aircraft exports.
    (d) Americans should do nothing but be happy that they can travel faster, partly at the expense of foreign taxpayers.

_____
*By April 1975 the choice between (b) and (d) had become a real issue as Britain and France sought permission for trans-Atlantic service to Washington and New York.

PROBLEM 20

THE CASE OF THE POPULATION BOMB

The gradual but relentless growth in world population is not literally a bomb. An organization warning against its hazards was more aptly named the "Campaign to Check the Population Explosion." Presumably the analogy with the hydrogen bomb is meant to suggest the future hazards for man himself in uncontrolled population growth, to say nothing of the already disastrous effects on many species of wildlife.

The general course of world population growth has been the following:

Year	Estimated Population	Average Percentage Change in a Year
8000 B.C.	10,000,000	
1 A.D.	300,000,000	0.05%
1650	500,000,000	0.05
1750	800,000,000	0.50
1850	1,250,000,000	0.50
1950	2,500,000,000	0.70
1970	3,600,000,000	1.80

The explosion started around the beginning of the eighteenth century. Mortality rates began to drop, particularly among young adults and children in the more economically advanced parts of the world. It gained intensity in the twentieth century, especially after World War II, as relatively simple public-health measures were extended to underdeveloped economies. The explosion has dampened somewhat by lower birth rates in economically advanced nations. In the United States, an estimated birth rate of over 50 per thousand between 1790 and 1820 dropped to 32 by 1900 and to about 17 in the 1930s. After a postwar rise to 25, it fell back to near 17 in the late 1960s. In 1973 the actual number of births had dropped below the long-run replacement level.

Also, some European countries can envision stable populations because the gradual aging of population would reduce birth rates and increase death rates to a position of equality before the year 2000. For the United States, where increases of over 1 percent a year seem likely for some time, important issues are those of the quality of life, such as the need of equal opportunities for slum children, the elimination of congestion and pollution, and the preservation of open spaces. Canada and Australia, now sparsely populated, are actively encouraging immigration to build population. For most of the world—Asia (except Japan, which has cut its birth rate per thousand from over 30 to less than 17 in 15 years), Africa, and Latin America—projection of immediate trends are different. With birth rates of 40 to 50 and death rates of 10 to 15, annual increases of 3 percent in population remain in prospect. Food production in these countries as a group has barely kept even with smaller population increases.

The table on the next page is presented for your analysis. It groups countries by literacy rates and compares this grouping with birth rates. It does not show the extent to which the "bomb" has been at least temporarily defused in the developed countries, particularly the United States, where the birth rate dropped to 15.1 per 1000 population by 1973 and 1974 and approximated the level of eventual zero population growth. The magnitude of the drop gained added significance since the proportion of population in the prime child-bearing ages was increasing as the result of the postwar baby boom.

Literacy Rate	Countries: Average Birth Rate per Thousand (1960-1964)							
IA 96-100%	Canada	25	Netherlands	21	France	18	Belgium	17
	USSR	23	Austria	19	West Germany	18	Czechoslovakia	16
	United States	22	United Kingdom	18	East Germany	18	Sweden	15
	Australia	22	Switzerland	18	Japan	17	Hungary	14
IB 76-95%	Chile	35	Argentina	22	Italy	19	Rumania	17
	Cuba	32	Yugoslavia	22	Greece	18		
	Spain	22	Poland	20	Bulgaria	17		
II 51-75%	Burma	50	Colombia	44	Taiwan	37	China	34
	Mexico	46	South Korea	41	Peru	35		
	Venezuela	45	North Korea	39	Thailand	34		
III 26-50%	Indonesia	43	Malaya	41	India	40		
	Brazil	43	Cambodia	41	Madagascar	38		
IV 1-25%	Ghana	56	Mozambique	47	Pakistan	45	Uganda	42
	Nigeria	49	Iran	46	U.A.R.	43	Congo	43
	Morocco	47	Nepal	45	Sudan	42	Algeria	39

The median population growth rates (1958-1963): Group I, 1.2 percent; Group II, 2.7 percent; Groups III and IV, 2.4 percent.

Source: This table is a substantial modification of data by B. Alfred Liu, "Population Growth and Education Development," *Annals of the American Academy of Political and Social Science* (January, 1967). The underlying figures are from United Nations publications.

Questions

1. Work out birth rate medians for each group. Group IA _____; Group IB _____; Group II _____; Group III _____; Group IV _____.

2. (a) Would you conclude that these data are consistent with the hypothesis that birth rates are inversely related with literacy rates?

   (b) What other factors might be behind both the rise in literacy and the lowered birth rates?

3. Keeping in mind that annual population increase is essentially determined by the birth rate minus the death rate (immigration or emigration is important in relatively few cases), why might the population increase in Group II be more than that of Groups III and IV?

4. Literacy is associated with many measures of economic progress, so the relationship above is not necessarily causal. Can you suggest any reasons for thinking that the conquest of illiteracy might help in reducing birth rates? Might it be a necessary but not sufficient condition?

5. Suppose that world population increased at an annual rate of 2.4 percent after 1970. Approximately when would world population reach 7.2 billion? _____ What would it be by the year 2150? _____

6. If birth rates do not decline, what will eventually check the growth of population?

7. (This question is for discussion only; simply note points.)
The task of transforming high-birth-rate and high-death-rate societies into low-birth-rate and low-death-rate societies is a difficult one, as was brought out in the United Nations Population Conference in Bucharest in the late summer of 1974. The U.S. position as expressed by Caspar Weinberger, the Secretary of Health, Education and Welfare, proposed an average limit of two children per family by the year 2000. U.N. Secretary-General Waldheim stressed the need for "immediate action" in the face of the "virtual certainty" of a world population of 8 billion by that year. Third-world nations argued against the high resource use and consumption levels of the Western nations and for a radical distribution of wealth as the important issue. Several countries such as Brazil and Rumania announced policies seeking higher national populations. Catholic spokesmen argued the inequities of artificial birth-control methods.
Consider the following courses of action for the United States and suggest a better one if possible:
(a) Encourage immigration to the level of several millions per year in an attempt to relieve overpopulation elsewhere.
(b) Agree to aim at redistributing income so that the poorest nations have at least one-third the standard of the richest.
(c) Tie economic aid, including food supplies, to significant attempts to get population growth under control.
(d) Do nothing on grounds that the population problem is essentially a national one or that the world is more likely to blow itself up before it starves.

PROBLEM 21

PRODUCTIVITY IN AGRICULTURE

	(1) Index of Farm Production (1967 = 100)	(2) Crop Production per Acre (1967 = 100)	(3) Man-hours of Farm Labor — Number (billions)	(4) Man-hours of Farm Labor — Index (1967 = 100)	(5) Index of Total Inputs (1967 = 100)	(6) Index of Fertilizer Input (1967 = 100)	(7) Index of Mechanical Power and Machinery (1967 = 100)
1929	53	57	23.2	302	99	11	40
1940	60	62	20.5	269	97	14	43
1950	73	69	15.1	190	100	32	80
1960	90	88	9.8	134	96	54	92
1970	102	102	6.5	89	101	113	101
1973	116	114	6.5	89	104	124	105

Sources: U.S. Department of Agriculture. Reported in *Economic Report of the President.*

(a) Why is column 2 the only productivity index?

(b) What might you conclude from the figures in columns 1 and 2 about the amount of land used for agriculture in 1973 compared with 1929?

(c) Between 1929 and 1973, agricultural production doubled and labor input decreased to substantially less than one-third of that of 1929. Therefore, labor productivity in agriculture in 1973 was more than _____ times as great as in 1929.

(d) What evidence is there above of the technological changes responsible for this?

(e) Why would it be misleading to say that overall productivity in agriculture increased over six times between 1929 and 1973 without specifying labor productivity?

(f) Using columns 1 and 4, construct a labor productivity index for agriculture (1967 = 100); 1929 _____; 1940 _____; 1950 _____; 1960 _____; 1970 _____; 1973 _____.

(g) Over what part of this period was the change so rapid as to suggest the term "revolution"?

(h) We have noted that two productivity measures have risen: labor productivity tremendously with labor inputs dropping; land productivity, as measured by crops per acre, moderately with land inputs fixed. But consider what has happened to fertilizer protivity by dividing column 1 (output) by column 6 (input) and multiplying by 100 to express series as an index.

1929	482	1960	_____
1940	_____	1970	_____
1950	_____	1973	_____

What are the probable reasons for this decline?

(i) How might the jump in the price of energy in the middle 1970s (fertilizer production and use account for about .5 percent of U.S. energy consumption) influence the measured productivity of fertilizer?

(j) What overriding influence are the increasing demands on fixed American agricultural land for food production likely to have on this measure of fertilizer productivity?

PROBLEM 22

POT EQUALS POLLUTION

The title for this problem suggests a simple framework for considering aspects of the growth controversy. P is taken as population, O as output per capita, and T as a technological variable to express how polluting are the methods used to produce or consume output. Pollution can be thought of as that of a particular type (such as sulfur dioxide in air, oxygen-consuming waste in water, solid waste) or more generally as a weighted index of all types of pollution, which of course would constitute a formidable measurement problem.

P, O, and T could all be expressed as having values of 1 in some base year plus a percentage addition to represent the annual growth rate. Thus pollution at the end of n years could be expressed as follows, for an economy in which the annual population growth was 1 percent, output per capita increased annually by 3 percent, and technology in respect to pollution was unchanging:

$$\text{pollution} = (1.01)^n (1.03)^n (1.00)^n$$

This formulation implies that pollution increases proportionally with the increase in total output (P x O) if technology is unchanging. This is not necessarily true. For example, much of the particulate matter in the air comes from volcanic discharges, so that a doubling of man-made output would less than double this form of pollution. On the other hand, because rivers have some natural cleansing powers, a doubling of output could more than double the level of oxygen-consuming discharges into rivers. A simple way out of this problem is to think of T as including the effect of these nonproportionalities.

In the formulation above, pollution would increase 16-fold in 72 years. (You should use the "rule of 72," which states that the doubling time is equal to 72 divided by the annual rate of growth. The derivation of this is shown.)

Questions

1. The annual population increase of 1 percent and per capita output increase of 3 percent are assumptions better suited to developed countries. Assume that 2 percent increases in each are appropriate for the world as a whole. Does this change the projection for pollution over 72 years as made above?

2. What assumption in either of these formulations of the model puts it in the "doomsday" class? What value would the T term have to have to prevent an increase in pollution?

3. Consider how these following interrelationships or developments would influence the variables above and thus the eventual projections for pollution:

(a) A switch back to the use of returnable bottles, with significant savings in the energy now used to make nonreturnable bottles, steel cans, and (in particular) aluminum cans.

(b) An increased death rate from respiratory diseases in infants and the elderly, associated with increased air pollution.

(c) The commitment of a $100 billion investment to complete the achievement of purer water standards (assume that this also decreases investment funds available for increasing output).

(d) The reduced death rate following initial increases in output for a very poor country.

(e) The reduced birth rate in a country well on its way to development.

4. The POT formulation does not incorporate prospective or actual famine. How might economies attempt to adjust to these threats in ways that might reduce the pollution threat? In ways that might increase it?

COSTS AND BENEFITS OVER TIME: PRESENT VALUE AND INTEREST

PROBLEM 23

THE PERFORMANCE OF SOME STOCKS AND BONDS

The table below contains the prices quoted for securities of five companies: American Telephone & Telegraph, Alcoa Aluminum, Fuqua Industries (a relatively new diversified growth company), Consolidated Edison (New York City electric utility), and the Southern Pacific Railroad.

The figure after the bonds is annual interest rate (bonds, although they are quoted as though the repayment were $100, are usually sold in $1,000 denominations), and the figure following the s (or series) denotes the year they are to be repaid. The figure after the stock prices represents annual dividends at the most recent rate as of late 1974.

BONDS

1968 Prices		Company	Contractual Interest	Year	Price	Interest on 1974 Price	Current
High	Low	Designation	(percent)	Due	10/20/74	(percent)	Price
74½	67½	Am T&T	3¼	s84	64½	5.0	
84½	78½	Alcoa	4¼	s82	74¼	5.7	
70	63⅛	Con Edis	2¾	s82	48	5.7	
89¾	83½	Fuqua Ind	7	s88	68½	10.2	
99⅞	96⅜	So Pac	4½	s69	Retired in 1969 at 100		

STOCKS

1968 Prices			1970 Annual Div.	1974 Annual Div.	Price	Dividend to 1974 Price	Current
High	Low	Companies	(in dollars)	(in dollars)	10/20/74	(percent)	Price
55¾	48	Am T&T	2.60	3.60	45½	7.9	
81½	62½	Alcoa	1.80	1.34	34⅜	3.9	
35½	31⅝	Con Edis	1.80	1.10	7¾	14.2	
45	32⅝	Fuqua Ind	.45[a]	—	4⅞	—	
42⅛	26¾	So Pac	2.00	2.24	28¾	7.8	

[a]Payable in stock in 1971.

Questions

1.   (a) Which group of securities, bonds or stocks, showed the greatest price volatility within 1968 and from 1968 to 1974?

     (b) Why would you expect this, given the characteristics of the two types of securities?

2.   (a) Compare the annual dividends as a percent of stock price with annual interest on bonds as a percent of their current prices for each company. (Figures for 1970 are given in the third-to-last column of the table.)

     (b) What features of bonds and stocks are compatible with this discrepancy considering the companies involved?

3.   Why might you surmise from the data given that Fuqua Industries was considered a risky investment with some potential for growth? What had apparently happened to feeling about this growth potential by 1974?

4.   Would you have been better off to have had a 5-percent savings deposit from mid-1968 to mid-1970 than to have invested in these bonds; in these stocks for the period? (Assume purchase price midway between high and low for 1968.)

5.   Look up the current prices of these securities in the financial pages of your newspaper. What would these bonds and stocks have given you in annual payments from 1968 or 1974 to date? In capital appreciation? In both together?

PROBLEM 24

PV, THE "IN" THING

The present-value tables are now "in." All over the nation, executives, bankers, and students are calculating the net discounted present values (PV) and rates of return as an aid to analyzing real investment and financial decisions. Work the following in full confidence that you are with the times.

We start with some exercises designed to familiarize use with the PV tables. Answers are given at end of problem.

A. Just for practice, fill in the following blanks using the table entitled Present Value of $1.00.

	This many $	in t years	has this PV	at i rate of interest
(a)	10	5	_____	6%
(b)	100	50	$60.80	_____
(c)	1,000	_____	3.00	12
(d)	_____	6	4.56	14

B. More practice, this time with the annuity table, Present Value of $1.00 Received Annually for t Years.

	This many $	received each year for t years	has this PV	at i rate of interest
(a)	10	5	_____	6%
(b)	100	50	$3,919.60	_____
(c)	1,000	_____	8,304.00	12
(d)	_____	6	38.89	14

C. From Table 22-1, discover for yourself the famous Rule of _____. The blank represents the number into which an interest rate (or any other rate of growth) is divided in order to get the number of years in which a magnitude will double at that rate of annual compound interest. What number belongs in the blank? (Hint: Find in each column the present value closest to 0.5; then multiply the associated year by the interest rate at the head of that column.)

1. *Sweetening the government bonds.* During World War II, Series E bonds sold at $18.75 and were redeemable at $25 in 10 years (this represented 3 percent interest). The government wished to preserve the magic numbers $18.75 and $25, so it decided to alter t when it became necessary to make the bonds more competitive with higher-interest securities in the 1950s and 1960s. Find the appropriate t to make the interest rate 4 percent: _____. To make the interest rate 6 percent: _____.

2. *Aging the Scotch.* In order to finance the aging of their whiskey, canny Scots offered rich Americans an opportunity for capital gains, which are taxed at lower rates than other income. They organized syndicates giving Americans the right to purchase newly distilled Scotch with an option to resell it to the syndicate in 8 years. (Scotch is usually bottled as 4, 8, or occasionally 12 years old.)

If you could buy 1,000 gallons at $1.00 a gallon and had the option to resell in 4 years for $1,250, approximately what interest rate would you receive? _____ What offer (approximate) should the syndicate make per 1,000 gallons for 8-year Scotch to maintain the same interest rate? _____

Table 22-1 Present Value of $1.00

$$PV = \left(\frac{1}{1+i}\right)^t$$

Years hence (t)	1%	2%	4%	6%	8%	10%	12%	14%	15%	16%	18%	20%	22%	24%	25%	26%	28%	30%	35%	40%	45%	50%
1	0.990	0.980	0.962	0.943	0.926	0.909	0.893	0.877	0.870	0.862	0.847	0.833	0.820	0.806	0.800	0.794	0.781	0.769	0.741	0.714	0.690	0.667
2	0.980	0.961	0.925	0.890	0.857	0.826	0.797	0.769	0.756	0.743	0.718	0.694	0.672	0.650	0.640	0.630	0.610	0.592	0.549	0.510	0.476	0.444
3	0.971	0.942	0.889	0.840	0.794	0.751	0.712	0.675	0.658	0.641	0.609	0.579	0.551	0.524	0.512	0.500	0.477	0.455	0.406	0.364	0.328	0.296
4	0.961	0.924	0.855	0.792	0.735	0.683	0.636	0.592	0.572	0.552	0.516	0.482	0.451	0.423	0.410	0.397	0.373	0.350	0.301	0.260	0.226	0.198
5	0.951	0.906	0.822	0.747	0.681	0.621	0.567	0.519	0.497	0.476	0.437	0.402	0.370	0.341	0.328	0.315	0.291	0.269	0.223	0.186	0.156	0.132
6	0.942	0.888	0.790	0.705	0.630	0.564	0.507	0.456	0.432	0.410	0.370	0.335	0.303	0.275	0.262	0.250	0.227	0.207	0.165	0.133	0.108	0.088
7	0.933	0.871	0.760	0.665	0.583	0.513	0.452	0.400	0.376	0.354	0.314	0.279	0.249	0.222	0.210	0.198	0.178	0.159	0.122	0.095	0.074	0.059
8	0.923	0.853	0.731	0.627	0.540	0.467	0.404	0.351	0.327	0.305	0.266	0.233	0.204	0.179	0.168	0.157	0.139	0.123	0.091	0.068	0.051	0.039
9	0.914	0.837	0.703	0.592	0.500	0.424	0.361	0.308	0.284	0.263	0.225	0.194	0.167	0.144	0.134	0.125	0.108	0.094	0.067	0.048	0.035	0.026
10	0.905	0.820	0.676	0.558	0.463	0.386	0.322	0.270	0.247	0.227	0.191	0.162	0.137	0.116	0.107	0.099	0.085	0.073	0.050	0.035	0.024	0.017
11	0.896	0.804	0.650	0.527	0.429	0.350	0.287	0.237	0.215	0.195	0.162	0.135	0.112	0.094	0.086	0.079	0.066	0.056	0.037	0.025	0.017	0.012
12	0.887	0.788	0.625	0.497	0.397	0.319	0.257	0.208	0.187	0.168	0.137	0.112	0.092	0.076	0.069	0.062	0.052	0.043	0.027	0.018	0.012	0.008
13	0.879	0.773	0.601	0.469	0.368	0.290	0.229	0.182	0.163	0.145	0.116	0.093	0.075	0.061	0.055	0.050	0.040	0.033	0.020	0.013	0.008	0.005
14	0.870	0.758	0.577	0.442	0.340	0.263	0.205	0.160	0.141	0.125	0.099	0.078	0.062	0.049	0.044	0.039	0.032	0.025	0.015	0.009	0.006	0.003
15	0.861	0.743	0.555	0.417	0.315	0.239	0.183	0.140	0.123	0.108	0.084	0.065	0.051	0.040	0.035	0.031	0.025	0.020	0.011	0.006	0.004	0.002
16	0.853	0.728	0.534	0.394	0.292	0.218	0.163	0.123	0.107	0.093	0.071	0.054	0.042	0.032	0.028	0.025	0.019	0.015	0.008	0.005	0.003	0.002
17	0.844	0.714	0.513	0.371	0.270	0.198	0.146	0.108	0.093	0.080	0.060	0.045	0.034	0.026	0.023	0.020	0.015	0.012	0.006	0.003	0.002	0.001
18	0.836	0.700	0.494	0.350	0.250	0.180	0.130	0.095	0.081	0.069	0.051	0.038	0.028	0.021	0.018	0.016	0.012	0.009	0.005	0.002	0.001	0.001
19	0.828	0.686	0.475	0.331	0.232	0.164	0.116	0.083	0.070	0.060	0.043	0.031	0.023	0.017	0.014	0.012	0.009	0.007	0.003	0.002	0.001	
20	0.820	0.673	0.456	0.312	0.215	0.149	0.104	0.073	0.061	0.051	0.037	0.026	0.019	0.014	0.012	0.010	0.007	0.005	0.002	0.001	0.001	
21	0.811	0.660	0.439	0.294	0.199	0.135	0.093	0.064	0.053	0.044	0.031	0.022	0.015	0.011	0.009	0.008	0.006	0.004	0.002	0.001		
22	0.803	0.647	0.422	0.278	0.184	0.123	0.083	0.056	0.046	0.038	0.026	0.018	0.013	0.009	0.007	0.006	0.004	0.003	0.001	0.001		
23	0.795	0.634	0.406	0.262	0.170	0.112	0.074	0.049	0.040	0.033	0.022	0.015	0.010	0.007	0.006	0.005	0.003	0.002	0.001			
24	0.788	0.622	0.390	0.247	0.158	0.102	0.066	0.043	0.035	0.028	0.019	0.013	0.008	0.006	0.005	0.004	0.003	0.002	0.001			
25	0.780	0.610	0.375	0.233	0.146	0.092	0.059	0.038	0.030	0.024	0.016	0.010	0.007	0.005	0.004	0.003	0.002	0.001	0.001			
26	0.772	0.598	0.361	0.220	0.135	0.084	0.053	0.033	0.026	0.021	0.014	0.009	0.006	0.004	0.003	0.002	0.002	0.001				
27	0.764	0.586	0.347	0.207	0.125	0.076	0.047	0.029	0.023	0.018	0.011	0.007	0.005	0.003	0.002	0.002	0.001	0.001				
28	0.757	0.574	0.333	0.196	0.116	0.069	0.042	0.026	0.020	0.016	0.010	0.006	0.004	0.002	0.002	0.002	0.001	0.001				
29	0.749	0.563	0.321	0.185	0.107	0.063	0.037	0.022	0.017	0.014	0.008	0.005	0.003	0.002	0.002	0.001	0.001					
30	0.742	0.552	0.308	0.174	0.099	0.057	0.033	0.020	0.015	0.012	0.007	0.004	0.003	0.002	0.001	0.001	0.001					
40	0.672	0.453	0.208	0.097	0.046	0.022	0.011	0.005	0.004	0.003	0.001	0.001										
50	0.608	0.372	0.141	0.054	0.021	0.009	0.003	0.001	0.001	0.001												

Table 22-2 Present Value of $1.00 Received Annually for t Years

$$PV = \left(\frac{1}{1+i}\right)^1 + \left(\frac{1}{1+i}\right)^2 + \cdots + \left(\frac{1}{1+i}\right)^t$$

Years (t)	1%	2%	4%	6%	8%	10%	12%	14%	15%	16%	18%	20%	22%	24%	25%	26%	28%	30%	35%	40%	45%	50%
1	0.990	0.980	0.962	0.943	0.926	0.909	0.893	0.877	0.870	0.862	0.847	0.833	0.820	0.806	0.800	0.794	0.781	0.769	0.741	0.714	0.690	0.667
2	1.970	1.942	1.886	1.833	1.783	1.736	1.690	1.647	1.626	1.605	1.566	1.528	1.492	1.457	1.440	1.424	1.392	1.361	1.289	1.224	1.165	1.111
3	2.941	2.884	2.775	2.673	2.577	2.487	2.402	2.322	2.283	2.246	2.174	2.106	2.042	1.981	1.952	1.923	1.868	1.816	1.696	1.589	1.493	1.407
4	3.902	3.808	3.630	3.465	3.312	3.170	3.037	2.914	2.855	2.798	2.690	2.589	2.494	2.404	2.362	2.320	2.241	2.166	1.997	1.849	1.720	1.605
5	4.853	4.713	4.452	4.212	3.993	3.791	3.605	3.433	3.352	3.274	3.127	2.991	2.864	2.745	2.689	2.635	2.532	2.436	2.220	2.035	1.876	1.737
6	5.795	5.601	5.242	4.917	4.623	4.355	4.111	3.889	3.784	3.685	3.498	3.326	3.167	3.020	2.951	2.885	2.759	2.643	2.385	2.168	1.983	1.824
7	6.728	6.472	6.002	5.582	5.206	4.868	4.564	4.288	4.160	4.039	3.812	3.605	3.416	3.242	3.161	3.083	2.937	2.802	2.508	2.263	2.057	1.883
8	7.652	7.325	6.733	6.210	5.747	5.335	4.968	4.639	4.487	4.344	4.078	3.837	3.619	3.421	3.329	3.241	3.076	2.925	2.598	2.331	2.108	1.922
9	8.566	8.162	7.435	6.802	6.247	5.759	5.328	4.946	4.772	4.607	4.303	4.031	3.786	3.566	3.463	3.366	3.184	3.019	2.665	2.379	2.144	1.948
10	9.714	8.983	8.111	7.360	6.710	6.145	5.650	5.216	5.019	4.833	4.494	4.192	3.923	3.682	3.571	3.465	3.269	3.092	2.715	2.414	2.168	1.965
11	10.368	9.787	8.760	7.877	7.139	6.495	5.988	5.453	5.234	5.029	4.656	4.327	4.035	3.776	3.656	3.544	3.335	3.147	2.757	2.438	2.185	1.977
12	11.255	10.575	9.385	8.384	7.536	6.814	6.194	5.660	5.421	5.197	4.793	4.439	4.127	3.851	3.725	3.606	3.387	3.190	2.779	2.456	2.196	1.985
13	12.134	11.343	9.986	8.853	7.904	7.103	6.424	5.842	5.583	5.342	4.910	4.533	4.203	3.912	3.780	3.656	3.427	3.223	2.799	2.468	2.204	1.990
14	13.004	12.106	10.563	9.295	8.244	7.367	6.628	6.002	5.724	5.468	5.008	4.611	4.265	3.962	3.824	3.695	3.459	3.249	2.814	2.477	2.210	1.993
15	13.865	12.849	11.118	9.712	8.559	7.606	6.811	6.142	5.847	5.575	5.092	4.675	4.315	4.001	3.859	3.726	3.483	3.268	2.825	2.484	2.214	1.995
16	14.718	13.578	11.652	10.106	8.851	7.824	6.974	6.265	5.954	5.669	5.162	4.730	4.357	4.003	3.887	3.751	3.503	3.283	2.834	2.489	2.216	1.997
17	15.562	14.292	12.166	10.477	9.122	8.022	7.120	6.373	6.047	5.749	5.222	4.775	4.391	4.059	3.910	3.771	3.518	3.295	2.840	2.492	2.218	1.998
18	16.398	14.992	12.659	10.828	9.372	8.201	7.250	6.467	6.128	5.818	5.273	4.812	4.419	4.080	3.928	3.786	3.529	3.304	2.844	2.494	2.219	1.999
19	17.226	15.678	13.134	11.158	9.604	8.365	7.366	6.550	6.198	5.877	5.316	4.844	4.442	4.097	3.942	3.799	3.539	3.311	2.848	2.496	2.220	1.999
20	18.046	16.351	13.590	11.470	9.818	8.514	7.469	6.623	6.259	5.929	5.353	4.870	4.460	4.110	3.954	3.808	3.546	3.316	2.850	2.497	2.221	1.999
21	18.857	17.011	14.029	11.764	10.017	8.649	7.562	6.687	6.312	5.973	5.384	4.891	4.476	4.121	3.963	3.816	3.551	3.320	2.852	2.498	2.221	2.000
22	19.660	17.658	14.451	12.042	10.201	8.772	7.645	6.743	6.359	6.011	5.410	4.909	4.488	4.130	3.970	3.822	3.556	3.323	2.853	2.498	2.222	2.000
23	20.456	18.292	14.857	12.303	10.371	8.883	7.718	6.792	6.399	6.044	5.432	4.925	4.499	4.137	3.976	3.827	3.559	3.325	2.854	2.499	2.222	2.000
24	21.243	18.914	15.247	12.550	10.529	8.985	7.784	6.835	6.434	6.073	5.451	4.937	4.507	4.143	3.981	3.831	3.562	3.327	2.855	2.499	2.222	2.000
25	22.023	19.523	15.622	12.783	10.675	9.077	7.843	6.873	6.464	6.097	5.467	4.948	4.514	4.147	3.985	3.834	3.564	3.329	2.856	2.499	2.222	2.000
26	22.795	20.121	15.983	13.003	10.810	9.161	7.896	6.906	6.491	6.118	5.480	4.956	4.520	4.151	3.988	3.837	3.566	3.330	2.856	2.500	2.222	2.000
27	23.560	20.707	16.330	13.211	10.935	9.237	7.943	6.935	6.514	6.136	5.492	4.964	4.524	4.154	3.990	3.839	3.567	3.331	2.856	2.500	2.222	2.000
28	24.316	21.281	16.663	13.406	11.051	9.307	7.984	6.961	6.534	6.152	5.502	4.970	4.528	4.157	3.992	3.840	3.568	3.331	2.857	2.500	2.222	2.000
29	25.066	21.844	16.984	13.591	11.158	9.370	8.022	6.983	6.551	6.166	5.510	4.975	4.531	4.159	3.994	3.841	3.569	3.332	2.857	2.500	2.222	2.000
30	25.808	22.306	17.292	13.765	11.258	9.427	8.055	7.003	6.566	6.177	5.517	4.979	4.534	4.160	3.995	3.842	3.569	3.332	2.857	2.500	2.222	2.000
40	32.835	27.355	19.793	15.046	11.925	9.779	8.244	7.105	6.642	6.234	5.548	4.997	4.544	4.166	3.999	3.846	3.571	3.333	2.857	2.500	2.222	2.000
50	39.196	31.424	21.482	15.762	12.234	9.915	8.304	7.133	6.661	6.246	5.554	4.999	4.545	4.167	4.000	3.846	3.571	3.333	2.857	2.500	2.222	2.000

3. *Dropping out with Dad*. Business executive R. P. Squarehole, after a vigorous discussion with R. P., Jr., is considering whether he should drop out of the establishment. He is 50 years old and has $100,000 and adequate pension rights at age 60. Would a 6-percent, 10-year annuity yield him the $13,500 a year he feels would make it feasible? (Note that such an annuity would provide equal payments, pay 6 percent on the declining balance, and exhaust his capital at the end of 10 years.)

4. *Calculating the net rate of return*. The Acme Machine Shop is analyzing a proposal to purchase labor-saving equipment estimated to save $15,000 a year less $1,000 maintenance. It calculates a 10-year life and $10,000 salvage value for the $75,000 machine. It wishes a return of 14 percent per year before taxes. Should it invest?

5. *Making sense out of bond prices*. In July, 1971, the following prices were quoted for certain corporate bonds:

Company	Coupon Rate (percent)	Year Repayable	Price (dollars)
Liggett & Myers	6%	1992	$ 81
Pacific Electric	8	2003	100
Atchison, Topeka & Santa Fe	4	1995	59
N.Y. Central (in bankruptcy)	6	1990	46

What was the approximate interest rate at the time?
Explain why the prices of bonds differed so greatly by showing that the interest rate was about the same for the bonds of all the solvent corporations above.

6. *My son, the doctor, maybe*. The senior Schmidts were considering with son Hermann whether he should go on to medical school or enter the family business. They estimated that if he went on to medical school (four years), internship (one year), and a residency for surgical training (four years), the opportunity cost would be $10,000 a year—mostly for reduced earnings for the nine years. It was estimated that from the tenth to the fortieth year, his earnings in medicine would exceed his business earnings by $10,000 a year. Mother Schmidt argued for the prestige of the M.D., but father wanted assurance that this investment in Hermann capital would yield at least 6 percent. Would it? What is it estimated to yield?

Answers to starting exercises: A. (a) $7.47 (b) 1% (c) 50 (d) 10; B. (a) $42.12 (b) 1 (c) 50 (d) 10; C. 72.

PROBLEM 25

THE COSTS OF COLLEGE FOR MR. AVERAGE GUY

It is well to acknowledge at the start that the answer to this problem is not definitive for any reader. The purpose is to deal with opportunity cost over time with present value techniques. No male chauvinism is intended by excluding women. Their changing participation and continuity in the labor force makes the use of earnings data that reflect past employment practices too unpresentative of the future.

Mr. A. G. has before him the following survey (May, 1973, Department of Labor).

Average Weekly Earnings of Males Who Worked Full Time,
(by age and years of schooling)

	Years of Schooling	
	12	16
20-24 years	$158	$170
25-34 years	201	238
35-44 years	226	317
45-54 years	227	347
55-64 years	227	323

In constructing the worksheet below, the following assumptions have been made:

1. That Mr. A. G. would enter either college or the full-time work force on his eighteenth birthday
2. That the differential in college and noncollege earnings would reflect those of the survey (these are rounded off and averaged for the 35-64 period)
3. That suitable interest rates to use would be 6%, an estimate of what could have been received in a savings account, and 8% to allow for greater risk
4. That he would earn $5000 less per year in college than outside and he would incur $2500 extra costs while in college (tuition, books, fees, etc.)

Fill in the blanks in the table below.

Age	Years	(A) College Earnings	(B) Non-college Earnings	A – B	Annuity Factor		NPV 6%	8%
18-21	1-4	(2,500)	5,000					
22-24	5-7	8,500	8,000					
25-34	8-17	12,000	10,000					
35-64	18-47	16,500	11,000					
Total								

Note: Use 15.59 and 12.16 as the interpolations for the PV of a $1 for 47 years. Thus the appropriate annuity factor for years 19-48 at 6% would be 15.59 - 10.48 = 5.11. Two decimal points represent sufficient accuracy.

Questions

1. Interpret the results of your calculations.

2. Consider critically the assumptions and then applicability to your own situation. For example, an obvious upward bias on the return to a college education is that the differential is attributed to college, whereas the talent and advantages of family position of the college group may influence earnings irrespective of the education. A less apparent downward bias is that, although the income curve of each age group rises steadily as it grows older, the survey table shows an apparent fall in income for ages 55-64 for college graduates, reflecting the experience of an age group that started on a lower income curve than that of younger groups.

PROBLEM 26

ECONOMICS FOR THE ENGINEER

Future engineers have a special concern for present-worth or -value problems for two reasons. First, the profession is necessarily involved in capital decisions in which resources are tied up over time in order that future benefits can be receied. This reason is a matter of degree, because virtually all of us will be concerned with some financial decisions such as taking out a mortgage; and many other careers in public administration, business, and banking require professional use of present-worth concepts. Second, more immediately, economic analysis questions on the professional engineers' examination are almost entirely confined to present-worth problems.

Most economics students can profit by examining representative problems from the professional engineering exam that follow, together with commentaries on solutions:

1. A dam was constructed for $200,000. The annual maintenance cost is $5,000. If interest is at 5%, the capitalized cost of the dam, including maintenance, is:
   (a) $100,000
   (b) $200,000
   (c) $215,000
   (d) $250,000
   (e) $300,000

Commentary. The capitalized cost is the present value of all costs, present and future. It equals $200,000 plus A/i where A has the standard meaning of equal annual payments or benefits for a future period which in this case is for practical purposes perpetual.

2. The modernization of a manufacturing plant is being considered. It has been ascertained that the present worth of the existing plant is $1,100,000 and has an estimated remaining life of 5 years and also that the salvage value of the plant at the end of this 5-year period would be $100,000. The investigation indicated that a new replacement plant located elsewhere would cost $3,350,000. The estimated life of this replacement plant would be 40 years and have a salvage value of $150,000. The annual operation and maintenance costs of the existing plant are $58,000, and that for the new replacement plant would be $42,600. Using the method of straight-line depreciation plus average interest and a 6% annual interest rate, determine the average annual costs for both the existing plant and the new plant. Also use financial method.

Commentary. In this problem we compute the annualized cost ( ) of the two alternatives because the lives are different. To compare the present worth of costs covering 40 years with those covering 5 years would obviously be fallacious. Because we are given the annual costs for operation and maintenance, this means that the capital recovery factor must be used. It has the formula $\dfrac{i(1 + i)^N}{(1 + i)^N - 1}$. Actually this is nothing more than the reciprocal of the present value of $1 received annually for N years. The second table in the PV case gives 1/4.212 for 5 years and 1/15.046 for 40 years. The simplest way to deal with the salvage value (which does not have to be recovered as an operating cost) is as a loan requiring 6% interest each year. Thus our comparison of the annualized costs of the two alternatives would be as follows:

	Old Plant		New Plant	
Operating and maintenance		$58,000		$42,600
Capital recovery	(1,000,000/4.212)		(3,200,000/15.046	
Interest on salvage	(100,000 x .06)		(150,000 x .06)	
Total				

This solution represents the "financial method" so named because of the importance of interest tables in such financial transactions as mortgages and annuities. The method of straight-line depreciation plus average interst (that is, interest on the average investment) does not require the use of tables.

The capital recovery costs are explicitly broken down into a depreciation and an interest component as follows: Depreciation is simply the present worth of the plant less the salvage with the difference divided by the years of life. For the new plant this would be $3,350,000 minus $150,000 equals $3,200,000 which divided by 40 gives $80,000 a year as the amount necessary to spread the erosion of capital equally over the plant's life. To find the average amount of capital resources tied up, the initial investment is added to the final investment and the sum divided by 2. For the new plant the answer is $1,750,000, which at 6% implies an average annual interest of $150,000. Work out the same costs for the old plant. The reason that the capital costs are less under this method is that the capital recovery factor provides for both depreciation and interest on that part of the investment that has not been recovered. This means that in the early years most of the cost represents interest so that the investment remaining unrecovered is substantially more than half of the initial investment. Mortgage payers are often dismayed to find out that after paying $1780 on a 30-year mortgage for $20,000 at 8% that they have reduced their indebtedness by only $180 rather than the $667 which would be one-thirtieth of the loan.

3. An old light-capacity highway bridge may be strengthened at a cost of $9,000, or it may be replaced by a new bridge of sufficient capacity at a cost of $40,000. The present net salvage value of the old bridge is $13,000. It is esimated that the old bridge, when reinforced, will last for 20 years, with a maintenance cost of $1,000 per year and have a salvage value of $10,000 at the end of 20 years. The estimated salvage value of the new bridge after 20 years of service is $15,000. The maintenance on the new bridge will be $100 per year. If interest is 6%, determine by the present-worth method whether it would be more economical to reinforce the old bridge or replace it.

Commentary. This is the find of problem in which the economist's way of thinking can simplify calculations for the engineer. The first step is to outline the time flow of costs and benefits for the two alternatives. The economist would then ask what is the additional investment required for the new bridge and what are the future benefits obtained by investing this extra capital. These can be obtained by subtracting the cash flow of the old bridge from that of the new bridge:

Year	0	1-20	20
New bridge	-27,000	- 100	+15,000
Old bridge	- 9,000	-1,000	+10,000
Additional investment and return			
	-18,000	+ 900	+ 5,000

The $13,000 salvage value for the old bridge is not a real opportunity cost for the old bridge, because the alternative of no bridge at all apparently does not exist. For the extra $18,000 the benefits are $900 in reduced maintenance for 20 years and a bonus of $5,000 in extra salvage at the end of the period. When we discount the benefits by 6%, we find that they are less than the $18,000 extra investment, so the old bridge is the more economically efficient. (The alternative method would require us to calculate the present values of costs for both the old and new bridge.) Confirm this solution, using the PV table.

The economist could then go further and derive a simple demand curve for capital from this problem. Nine thousand dollars of new investment would be demanded at a very high rate of interest (assuming the necessity of a functioning bridge); $27,000 would be demanded at a 2% rate of interest. Discover for yourself that the $18,000 in additional investment is approximately equal to the benefits when discounted by 2%.

PRICE DETERMINATION UNDER COMPETITION, MONOPOLISTIC COMPETITION, AND MONOPOLY

PROBLEM 27

ADAMS AND BROWN

Adams, Inc., and the Brown Company are 2 of 100 firms in the plastics-molding industry, in which equilibrium has been disturbed both by increases in demand and by new cost-saving techniques. Adams's costs reflect these.

Volume of Output (in thousands of units)	Adams				Brown			
	Total Cost	AVC	ATC	MC[b]	Total Cost	AVC	ATC	MC[b]
100	$100,000[a]	.20	1.00	.20	$ 60,000[a]	.30	.60	.30
200	120,000	.20	.60	.20	90,000	.30	.45	.30
300	140,000				120,000			
400	160,000				150,000			
500	180,000				180,000			
600	200,000				210,000			
700	220,000				250,000	.31	.36	.40
800	240,000				295,000			
900	270,000	.21	.30	.30	350,000	.36	.39	.55
1,000	310,000				N.A.			
1,100	N.A.				N.A.			

[a] Adams's fixed costs are $80,000; Brown's are $30,000.   N.A. = not attainable
[b] Remember to associate MC with the midpoints of volume intervals (preceding).

The current price for the product is $.35.

Questions

1. Graph below the ATC, AVC, and MC functions for the two firms, with the firm's demand curve reflecting the $.35 price. What output decision would you predict that Adams would make? _____ That Brown would make? _____

59

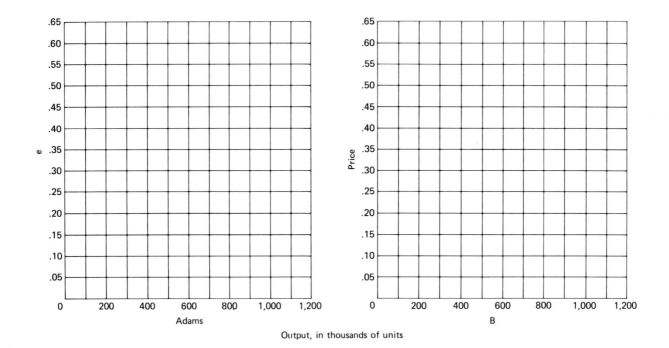

Output, in thousands of units

2. Assuming that 50 firms in the industry have costs identical to Adams and that 50 have costs identical to Brown, construct a short-run industry supply curve.

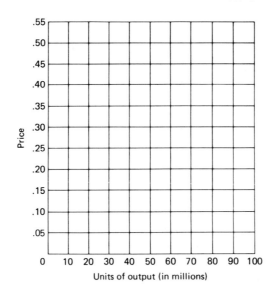

60

Price[a]	Amount Supplied		
	Adams	Brown	Industry (50A + 50B)
$.15	—	—	—
.20	750-800	—	37,500-40,000
.25			
.30			
.35			
.40			
.45			
.50			
.55			

[a]Treat each price as a shade above price listed.

3. Predict the long-run equilibrium price, assuming that the industry is one of constant costs and that the conditions of perfect competition regarding entry and exit are satisfied. _____ What kind of adjustments will firms of the Adams type need to make? Firms of the Brown type?

PROBLEM 28

PRICING EPISODES UNDER OLIGOPOLY
AND THE KINKED DEMAND CURVE

Although the kinked demand model often has been challenged on the grounds that frequently the price stability it predicts is not present, the combination of the complete-retaliation and no-retaliation demand curves provides a good framework for appraising actual behavior.

Questions

In each of the following incidents involving firms in oligopolistic industries, discuss briefly whether the behavior is consistent with kinked demand analysis, and if not, why that analysis has to be modified or is inappropriate in the particular instance.

1. On October 19, 1962, the Aluminum Company of America announced that it had rescinded a three-week-old one-cent-a-pound rise on uncoated, coiled, residential siding sheet. An Alcoa spokesman explained that the increase was withdrawn because no other producer followed the rise.

2. The newly formed Studebaker-Packard Corporation announced substantial price cuts on its 1955 Studebaker line in issuing their list of "Dynamic Factory Delivered Prices." Studebaker's share of the market had dropped from a postwar peak of 4 percent to about 1.5 percent in 1954, when sales were expected to run somewhat less than 100,000 cars. A letter to stockholders on November 22, 1954, after noting more powerful engines and styling leadership, stated:

Above all, may we call your attention to the prices that have been placed on the new Studebakers. With the various models ranging from $30 to $287 under the 1954 levels, Studebaker, the premium car, is now available without a premium cost. This "dynamic pricing"—pricing in anticipation of increased volume—is part of our program to meet the highly competitive conditions of the industry by becoming competitive in price.

3. "We're going out for the mass market as we never went after it before." So an RCA Victor official sums up the news that threw the phonograph record industry into turmoil this week. Starting January 3, Victor is whacking prices as much as 40 percent on some records, 33 percent on its 12-inch classical long-players, and smaller amounts on its 45-rpm records. The price of 78's—fast becoming obsolete—was raised from 89¢ to 98¢.

There is no reason to believe that Victor's cuts were a distress move. Record sales in 1954 topped 1953 by an estimated 5 percent to 20 percent. RCA Victor is convinced that the mass market is ripe for a real assault. The oncoming crop of teenagers (good buyers of popular records); the burgeoning of good, moderately priced turntables; the interest in high fidelity, all shore up the company's confidence. *(Business Week,* January 1, 1955)

RCA was said to hope for a doubling of sales (presumably in units), and some early reports were of a 100 percent increase in volume. Within a month the other major firms followed the price cuts, though not on all lines. *(Variety,* February 23, 1955)

4. *Business Week* (September 29, 1968) reported that the automobile pricing drama has followed the pattern of recent years: First, there was a rumor in the spring about a coming increase, this time $100. Then came Chrysler's announcement of its 1969 model prices (up $89 a car, or an estimated 2.9 percent), which seemed high and drew immediate criticism from Washington. Then came General Motors' lower price adjustment (an average increase of $52), which seemed mild by comparison. GM's Chairman Roche argued that cost increases for 1969 cars are considerably above the 1.6 percent price increase because labor increases exceeded any measurable rise in productivity and materials went up, steel by 6.3 percent. President Johnson praised the move as an act of moderation, and a few days later Chrysler cut back its increase to an average of $50, the same as reported by Ford. This represented the third successive readjustment by Chrysler for part of an announced price increase.

PROBLEM 29

YOU BE THE ANTITRUST JUDGE
OF THE ALLEGED CELLOPHANE MONOPOLY

The Antitrust Suit

The United States filed a complaint against the Du Pont Company in December, 1947, charging it with monopolizing, attempting to monopolize, and conspiring to monopolize interstate commerce in cellophane, all violations of Section 2 of the Sherman Act. The suit, a civil one, sought relief by injunction and by actions such as divestiture to dissipate the effect of monopolization. On Du Pont's motion, the case was transferred from the District of Columbia to the District of Delaware.

Judge Leahy's decision for the District Court was a lengthy one, winnowing out some 854 findings of fact out of 7,500 pages of testimony and 7,000 exhibits. He found for the defendants, and the government appealed the decision to the Supreme Court. After hearing the case in October, 1955, the Supreme Court found itself closely split. Imagine that you have the deciding vote.

The Basic History

In 1923, Du Pont and La Cellophane, a subsidiary of a French company that was the sole manufacturer of cellophane, organized an American company for the manufacture of cellophane. Du Pont received the exclusive rights to make and sell cellophane under the patents and secret processes of the French company in North and Central America. Du Pont bought the minority 48 percent stock interest of La Cellophane in the subsidiary in 1929 in exchange for stock valued at $90,000,000.

Du Pont embarked on a program of product improvement, price reduction, and output expansion in which the 1924 production of 361,249 pounds sold at an average price of $2.508 increased to 202,826,066 pounds sold at an average price of 49 cents in 1950. The most important product improvement was through a basic patent covering moisture-proof cellophane developed by 1927. Substantial expenditures on technical activities including process and quality improvement continued and amounted to $2,782,706 in 1950.

From 1925 to 1928, imports from a new Belgian plant, Societe Industrielle de la Cellulose (SIDAC), amounted to as much as 24 percent of the market, but a rise in tariffs (for which Du Pont was an influential lobbyist) prevented imports from again being an important factor. SIDAC, however, established an American competitor, the Sylvania Industrial Corporation, which completed a plant in Virginia in 1930. Du Pont regarded Sylvania's process for producing moisture-proof cellophane as an infringement and brought suit. The settlement agreed upon gave Sylvania a nonexclusive license on basic patents for a royalty of 2 percent of net cellophane sales under the patents. Provision for the cross-licensing of future patents was made. But the settlement also provided that Sylvania should pay a penalty royalty of 20 cents a pound if its production exceeded 20 percent of total moisture-proof sales. This percentage was to rise by 1 percent a year until it reached 29 percent in 1942. Sylvania never reached the quota and averaged about 23 percent of the market from 1933 to 1945. This share increased by only 1 percent after the expiration of the agreement in 1945 and the sale of Sylvania to American Viscose in 1946.

After the antitrust suit was filed in 1947, Du Pont actively sought out another firm to enter the field with its technical assistance and found a willing entrant in Olin Industries. After Olin's plant went into production in 1951, Du Pont's share of cellophane capacity was reduced to about 68 percent.

The Strategies of the Two Contenders

The government's basic strategy was a simple one. It sought to show that Du Pont had a dominant enough position in cellophane to constitute a monopoly with the power to control prices and exclude competitors. It counted on the 75 percent plus share of the market plus the restrictions on the only other producer to establish its dominance. It felt amply prepared to demonstrate that this dominance was not "thrust upon Du Pont" but was actively enough sought to constitute "monopolizing." The latter step could be well documented by Du Pont's maneuvers in getting and protecting exclusive rights in the U.S. market.

Du Pont's strategy was to swamp the government's case in market facts and to "demonstrate that Du Pont cellophane is sold under such competitive conditions that acquisition of market control or monopoly power is a practical impossibility." It aimed to show that Du Pont was competing in a broader market, "the flexible packaging materials market." Under able legal leadership, it made an all-out effort to gather market evidence, spending in excess of a million dollars for information on the customers of packaging converters.

Basic Market Facts Presented

Little justice can be done to 7,000 pages of evidence, but the following notes are sufficient:

Sales and Wholesale Prices of Flexible Wrapping Materials in 1949

	Thousands of Square Yards	Price, 1949[a]
Glassine, greaseproof and vegetable parchment papers	3,125,826	.9-1.4
Waxing papers (18 pounds and over)	4,614,685	1.1
Sulphite bag and wrapping papers	1,788,615	b
Aluminum foil	1,317,807	1.8
Cellophane	3,366,068	2.1-2.3
Cellulose acetate	133,982	3.3
Pliofilm, polyethylene, Saran, and Cry-O-Rap	373,871	3.8-6.1
Total	14,720,854	
Total Du Pont cellophane production	2,629,747	
Du Pont cellophane percent of total U.S. production and imports of these flexible packaging materials	17.9%	

[a] In cents per 1,000 square inches.
[b] Not available, but substantially lower than .7 cent.

Du Pont 1949 sales of cellophane, by percent devoted to various uses:

Tobacco products	14.3
Food products	67.7
Miscellaneous	15.3
Export	2.7

Du Pont also presented evidence about food products markets showing that according to converter's sales, cellophane had less than 50 percent of virtually all food products wrapping. The three leading categories follow:

	Cellophane Share (percent)	Leading Competitor (percent)	
Bakery products	7	Papers	88
Candy	24	Aluminum foil	33
Snacks	35	Glassine	63

Typical testimony on this point by a glassine manufacturer is the following:

> There is terrific competition now going on in bread and in the bake field, and as I mentioned before, potato chips; the snack specialty field, of which Fritos (indicating) are an example. It is all the time in a state of flux; we lose them, we get them back. The same thing happens with cellophane. Frankly, almost any one of these barrier jobs here is a competing point, as you see. Even in cereal we have to compete with a cellophane because a fellow can put his stuff up in a duplex cellophane bag or a waxed paper barrier of some sort. It is a choice he has to make. . . .

Facts were presented on physical qualities of various wrapping materials, for example on the following:

	Moisture-proof Cellophane	Waxed Paper	Glassine	Foil
Transparency	High	Medium	Medium	Opaque
Bursting strength	High	Good	Low	Low
Printability	Yes	Yes	Yes	Yes
Permeability to gases	Very low	Low	Low	Very low
Tear strength	Low	High	Good	Low

*Excerpts from the Opinion for Acquittal**

". . . If cellophane is the 'market' that du Pont is found to dominate, it may be assumed it does have monopoly power over that 'market.' Monopoly power is the power to control prices or exclude competition. It seems apparent that du Pont's power to set the price of cellophane has been limited only by the competition afforded by other flexible packaging materials. Moreover, it may be practically impossible for anyone to commence manufacturing cellophane without access to du Pont's technique. However, du Pont has no power to prevent competition from other wrapping materials. . . .

". . . But where there are market alternatives that buyers may readily use for their purposes, illegal monopoly does not exist merely because the product said to be monopolized differs from others. If it were not so, only physically identical products would be a part of the market. To accept the Government's argument, we would have to conclude that the manufacturers of plain as well as moisture-proof cellophane were monopolists, and so with films such as Pliofilm, foil, glassine, polyethylene, and Saran, for each of these wrapping materials is distinguishable. These were all exhibits in the case. New wrappings appear, generally similar to cellophane: is each a monopoly? What is called for is an appraisal of the 'cross-elasticity' of demand in the trade. . . .

". . . Cellophane costs more than many competing products and less than a few. But whatever the price, there are various flexible wrapping materials that are bought by manufacturers for packaging their goods in their own plants or are sold to converters who shape and print them for use in the packaging of the commodities to be wrapped. . . .

". . . It may be admitted that cellophane combines the desirable elements of transparency, strength and cheapness more definitely than any of the others. . . .

". . . But despite cellophane's advantages it has to meet competition from other materials in every one of its uses. . . .

". . . The over-all result is that cellophane accounts for 17.9% of flexible wrapping materials, measured by the wrapping surface. . . .

". . . An element for consideration as to cross-elasticity of demand between products is the responsiveness of the sales of one product to price changes of the other. If a slight decrease in the price of cellophane causes a considerable number of customers of other flexible wrappings to switch to cellophane, it would be an indication that a high cross-elasticity of demand exists between them; that the products compete in the same market. The court below held

---

*The pages that follow are taken from the trial record of U.S. v. E. I. du Pont de Nemours and Company, 3Jl U.S. 377 (1956).

that the 'great sensitivity of customers in the flexible packaging markets to price or quality changes' prevented du Pont from possessing monopoly control over price. . . .

". . . We conclude that cellophane's interchangeability with the other materials mentioned suffices to make it a part of this flexible packaging material market. . . .

". . . The facts above considered dispose also of any contention that competitors have been excluded by du Pont from the packaging material market. That market has many producers, and there is no proof du Pont ever has possessed power to exclude any of them from the rapidly expanding flexible packaging market. . . .

". . . Nor can we say that du Pont's profits, while liberal (according to the Government 15.9% net after taxes on the 1937-1947 average), demonstrate the existence of a monopoly without out proof of lack of comparable profits during those years in other prosperous industries. . . ."

Excerpts from the Opinion for Conviction

". . . This case, like many under the Sherman Act, turns upon the proper definition of the market. In defining the market in which du Pont's economic power is to be measured, the opposition virtually emasculates Section 2 of the Sherman Act. They admit that 'cellophane combines the desirable elements of transparency, strength and cheapness more definitely than any of' a host of other packaging materials. Yet they hold that all of those materials are so indistinguishable from cellophane as to warrant their inclusion in the market. . . .

". . . If the conduct of buyers indicated that glassine, waxed and sulphite papers, and aluminum foil were actually 'the selfsame products' as cellophane, the qualitative differences demonstrated by the comparison of physical properties would not be conclusive. But the record provides convincing proof that business men did not so regard these products. During the period covered by the complaint (1923-1947) cellophane enjoyed phenomenal growth. Do Pont's 1924 production was 361,249 pounds, which sold for $1,306,662. Its 1947 production was 133,502,858 pounds which sold for $55,339,626. Yet throughout this period the price of cellophane was far greater than that of glassine, waxed paper or sulphite paper. In 1929 cellophane's price was seven times that of glassine; in 1934, four times; and in 1949 still more than twice glassine's price. Cellophane had a similar price relation to waxed paper and sulphite paper sold at even less than glassine and waxed paper. We cannot believe that buyers, practical businessmen, would have bought cellophane in increasing amounts over a quarter of a century if close substitutes were available at from one-seventh to one-half cellophane's price. That they did so is testimony to cellophane's distinctiveness. . . .

". . . Sylvania, the only other cellophane producer, absolutely and immediately followed every du Pont price change, even dating back its price list to the effective date of du Pont's change. Producers of glassine and waxed paper, on the other hand, displayed apparent indifference to du Pont's repeated and substantial price cuts. From 1924 to 1932 du Pont dropped the price of plain cellophane 84%, while the price of glassine remained constant. And during the period 1933-1946 the prices for glassine and waxed paper actually increased in the face of a further 21% decline in the price of cellophane. If 'shifts of business' due to 'price sensitivity' had been substantial, glassine and waxed paper producers who wanted to stay in business would have been compelled by market forces to meet du Pont's price challenge just as Sylvania was. The opposition correctly point out that:

> An element for consideration as to cross-elasticity of demand between products is the responsiveness of the sales of one product to price changes of the other. If a slight decrease in the price of cellophane causes a considerable number of customers of other flexible wrappings to switch to cellophane, it would be an indication that a high cross-elasticity of demand exists between them; that the products compete in the same market.

Surely there was more than a 'slight decrease in the price of cellophane' during the period covered by the complaint. That producers of glassine and waxed paper remained dominant in the flexible packaging materials market without meeting cellophane's tremendous price cuts convinces us that cellophane was not in effective competition with their products. . . .

". . . When du Pont was contemplating entry into cellophane production, its Development Department reported that glassine 'is so inferior that it belongs in an entirely different class and has hardly to be considered as a competitor of cellophane.' This was still du Pont's view in 1950 when its survey of competitive prospects wholly omitted references to glassine, waxed paper, or sulphite paper and stated that 'Competition for du Pont cellophane will come from competitive cellophane and from noncellophane films made by us or by others.'

". . . As predicted by its 1923 market analysis, du Pont's dominance in cellophane proved enormously profitable from the outset. . . .

". . . But such success was not limited to the period of innovation, limited sales and complete domestic monopoly. A confidential du Pont report shows that during the period 1937-1947, despite great expansion of sales, du Pont's 'operative return' (before taxes) averaged 31 percent, while its average 'net return' (after deduction of taxes, bonuses, and fundamental research expenditure) was 15.9%. Such profits provide a powerful incentive for the entry of competitors. Yet from 1924-1951 only one new firm, Sylvania, was able to begin cellophane production. And Sylvania could not have entered if La Cellophane's secret process had not been stolen. It is significant that for 15 years Olin Industries, a substantial firm, was unsuccessful in its attempt to produce cellophane, finally abandoning the project in 1944 after having spent about $1,000,000. When the Government brought this suit, du Pont, 'To reduce the hazard of being judged to have a monopoly of the U.S. cellophane business,' decided to let Olin enter the industry.

"The trial judge thought that, if du Pont raised its price, the market would 'penalize' it with smaller profits as well as lower sales. Du Pont proved him wrong. When 1947 operating earnings dropped below 26% for the first time in 10 years, it increased cellophane's price 7% and boosted its earnings in 1948. Du Pont's division manager then reported that 'If an operative return of 31% is considered inadequate then an upward revision in prices will be necessary to improve the return.' It is this latitude with respect to price, this broad power of choice, that the antitrust laws forbid. Du Pont's independent pricing policy and the great profits consistently yielded by that policy leave no room for doubt that it had power to control the price of cellophane. The findings of fact cited by the majority cannot affect this conclusion. For they merely demonstrate that, during the period covered by the complaint, du Pont was a 'good monopolist,' i.e., that it did not engage in predatory practices and that it chose to maximize profits by lowering price and expanding sales. Proof of enlightened exercise of monopoly power certainly does not refute the existence of that power.

"The foregoing analysis of the record shows conclusively that cellophane is the relevant market. Since du Pont has the lion's share of that market, it must have monopoly power, as the majority concede. This being so, we think it clear that, in the circumstances of this case, du Pont is guilty of 'monopolization.'

"If competition is at the core of the Sherman Act, we cannot agree that it was consistent with that Act for the enormously lucrative cellophane industry to have no more than two sellers from 1924 to 1951. The conduct of du Pont and Sylvania illustrates that a few sellers tend to act like one and that an industry which does not have a competitive structure will not have competitive behavior. The public should not be left to rely upon the dispensations of management in order to obtain the benefits which normally accompany competition. Such beneficence is of uncertain tenure. Only actual competition can assure long-run enjoyment of the goals of a free economy."

Concluding Note

Between the time the case was brought in 1947 and the time of the decision in 1955, a trend had set in toward increased sales of other films, particularly polyethylene but also the polyvinyls and others. By the mid-1960s, polyethylene films alone exceeded cellophane sales substantially. Do you think these developments would influence your decision in the case? Why or why not?

Suggested Approach to the Case

In making your judgment, you should find it helpful to draw up a table showing the contrasting pictures of structure of the market as seen by the two opinions. Include the number of firms, share of market, independence of firms, and entry conditions. You should also have assessed the arguments on "cross-elasticity" and "good monopolist."

PROBLEM 30

THE MOUNTAIN DOCTOR

In 1965, Dr. Lawrence practiced in a remote mountain region over 50 miles from other medical services. To cover his family living expenditures and the fixed overhead expenses connected with his modest clinic required $20,000 gross income. (This amount was below the income he might command elsewhere but would be adequate.) In addition, he had expenses associated with visits estimated at $1.00 a visit. (This common unit, a visit, represents, of course, a considerable simplification of the variety of medical services he provided.)

The population of the area could be roughly divided into two groups. The first consisted of relatively prosperous merchants, ranchers, some executives, and vacationers and retired persons who enjoyed the rural way of life. The second, a lower-income group, included miners whose employment was irregular and somewhat marginal farmers.

Assume that the demand for Dr. Lawrence's services is described by smoothly drawn curves through the points given in the table and that Dr. Lawrence can provide a maximum of 5,000 visits per year.

Hypothetical Demand Schedule for Dr. Lawrence's Services

Fee	Group I Visits	Group II Visits	Total Visits
$25	300	0	300
20	500	0	500
15	700	200	900
10	900	800	1,700
5	1,100	2,000	3,100
0	1,300	3,700	5,000

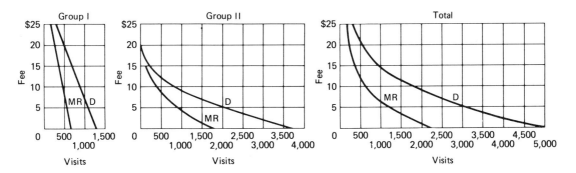

Note: The MR curves were plotted at interval midpoints as follows:
Group I: $12.50 at an output of 400, $2.50 at 600, -$7.50 at 800.
Group II: $15.00 at 100, $8.33 at 500, $1.67 at 1,400.
Total: $8.75 at 700, $4.38 at 1,300, -$1.07 at 2,400.

Interested students may wish to work out reasons for this.

69

1. Evaluate the following pricing alternatives by the criteria below. To size up Dr. Lawrence's problem, draw the long-run average cost curve on the "total" graph, and to help in the evaluations draw the MC curve on all three diagrams.

	Price(s)	Output	TR	TVC	TC	TR – TC
(a) One-price system	———	———	———	———	———	———
(b) Two-price system						
I	———	———	———	———	xxx	xxx
II	———	———	———	———	xxx	xxx
Total	xxx	———	———	———	———	———
(c) Perfect price from	———	———	———	———	———	———
discrimination to	———	———	———	———	———	———

(approximate total revenue from area under total demand curve on graph)

2. Recognizing that none of the alternatives above is fully possible [Dr. Lawrence would not have the perfect knowledge required for (c) and would find it professionally difficult to practice (a) and (b) without providing some free services and lower fees as well], what approach would you recommend?

3. Price discrimination in medical services probably has declined because of government programs.

    (a) Some communities have subsidized the building of a clinic. How would this affect Dr. Lawrence's problem?

    (b) How would the provision of government payments of minimum fees under Medicare (to the old) and Medicaid (to the poor) alter the demand and reduce the necessity for discrimination?

NONPRICE COMPETITION AND CORPORATE
SOCIAL RESPONSIBILITY

THE COSTS OF THE HORSEPOWER RACE
AND ANNUAL AUTOMOBILE STYLE CHANGES

It may seem quaint in the 1970s to dwell on the fact that not so long ago—in the 1950s—the automobile was a status symbol and that almost every year the automobile companies found it profitable to change models substantially each year to those of greater size and horsepower. Now, or at least in 1974, the hot cars are the Vega, the Pinto, the Datsun, the Toyota, and the Volkswagen, none noted for horsepower or size. Much of the change from year to year now is in safety features and pollution-control devices (under prodding by various governments). The high-powered, so-called "muscle" models of the mid-1960s have but fractions of their previous market shares.

But there was a time in the early 1960s when three economists* thought it important to ask how valuable were the resources that were committed to annual style changes and to the increase in size and horsepower during the 1950s. To use their words, "As there was technological change in the industry, we are thus assessing not the research expenditure that would have been saved if the 1949 models themselves had been continued but rather the resource expenditure that would have been saved had cars with 1949 specifications been continued but built with the developing technology. . . ."

Their findings expressed as average excessive costs per car for 1956-1960 period were as follows:

$454 for size and horsepower
$116 for optional equipment
$ 14 for advertising
$ 99 for retooling expenditures each year

The total of almost $700 per car was over 25 percent of the purchase price and amounted to $3,900,000,000 a year. In addition, gasoline bills were higher. With the improvement of technology, estimates for 1949 horsepower indicated that mileage could have risen from 16.4 to 18 miles per gallon. In fact, it fell to 14.3 miles per gallon. Thus, the owners were paying about 25 percent extra in gas costs ($40 for each 10,000 miles), and for the remaining years of the life of their cars faced the same higher bills. Including gasoline, the annual bill was estimated at over $5 billion a year (over 1 percent of GNP) for the period, a figure "so staggeringly high that it seems worthwhile presenting the bill and asking whether it was 'worth it.'" The authors did not deny that model changes brought benefits. They stated, "It is quite clear that most of all of the changes involved were in fact desired by the consuming

---

*See Franklin M. Fisher, Zvi Griliches, and Carl Kaysen, "The Costs of Automobile Model Changes Since 1949," *American Economic Review* (May, 1962), pp. 259-261.

public (perhaps after advertising) and that the automobile companies were satisfying such desire." (Such small cars as the Crosley, the Henry J, and the Hudson Hornet were rejected during the period, and only in 1960-1961 did the swing to compacts gain momentum.)

Questions

1. Do you believe automobile companies give the public the kinds of cars they want? Explain.

2. To the "consumerist" movement of the 1970s is it enough that purchasers get what they desire? Is it important that they get what they desire?

3. What are your theories about why the horsepower and size race became less important? How might your hypotheses be tested?

PROBLEM 32

REFRIGERATORS AND KWH'S

The sale of home refrigerators in the United States has been dominated by three firms in the postwar period—Sears (the Coldspot brand manufactured by Whirlpool), General Electric (Hotpoint brand), and General Motors (Frigidaire)—with a collective share averaging 60 percent. Price and product competition has been vigorous, with market surveys indicating that price per cubic foot has been the most important, with such features of no-frost operation and automatic ice makers a second important basis for brand choice. The performance of the industry and its products between 1958-1957 and 1972 had many exemplary aspects:

1. The price of the average refrigerator dropped from $320 to $290 when most prices were rising. Because the later refrigerators were larger, the cost per cubic foot of storage space dropped to 56 percent of the 1959 figure.
2. Service calls had been cut to less than half; "pulldown," the ability to cool rapidly, had increased materially; less room was needed per unit of usable space.
3. The proportion of low-temperature freezing space had increased, and features such as those indicated above had been added.

In one respect, however, the average new refrigerator of the early 1970s was distinctly more expensive than that of the 1950s: The average consumption of electricity had increased from just over 1 to 4 kilowatt-hours a day. Household refrigeration had come to account for about 6 percent of the total electricity usage in the United States.

The Center for Policy Alternatives at M.I.T. conducted a study of the life-cycle costs of the new and older refrigerators. In the study's opinion, "In spite of the lower cost of manual-defrost machines with their inconveniently small refrigerator volumes, it would seem to be an exercise in futility to try to promote a return to the horse-and-buggy days of the refrigerator business."* It therefore made estimates of engineering changes that could be made in the building of refrigerators that, while adding to the purchase price, would decrease energy use.

A comparison of the annualized life-cycle costs for four actual and hypothetical refrigerators is given below. A lifetime of 14 years is assumed for all four, and an interest rate of 8% is used to get an annual sum needed to amortize the purchase price (see the second table in "PV, the 'In' Thing" to get the 8.244 by which the purchase price was divided). The cut of $12 in service and maintenance costs for the no-frost refrigerator is largely an allowance for the saving of the consumer's time in defrosting and cleaning. The energy cost is computed from the usage as given at a price of $.03 per kilowatt-hour, a figure appropriate for 1972 before the most rapid escalation in electricity prices. All four models are 15 cubic feet in capacity, an average size for the early 1970s but far larger than the typical refrigerator of the late 1950s.

	(1) "Early" Model	(2) 1972 Model	(3) Improved 1972 Model A	(4) Improved 1972 Model B
Purchase price	($270)	($270)	($304)	($360)
Annual cost of A at 8%	33	33	37	48
Service/maintenance	25	13	13	13
Energy usage (kwhs/yr)	(790)	(1840)	(1215)	(950)
Energy cost (3¢/kwh)	$24	$55	$36	$29
Total annual costs	$82	$101	$86	$90

---

*The Productivity of Servicing Consumer Durable Products (1974), p. 182.

The "early" model (1) has manual defrost and only one-third the freezer capacity of the others (1.5 as compared with 4.5 cubic feet). The actual 1972 model (2) is "no-frost." The improved model A (3) substitutes polyurethane for glass fiber insulation and uses a more efficient compressor motor, adding an estimated $34 to the purchase price. The improved model B (4), in addition, has other engineering changes and costs $56 more.

Questions

1. Assuming that energy prices double to $.06 per kilowatt-hour, an event which has already taken place in some areas, which model(s) would rational consumers purchase? Will they necessarily do so?

2. Which of the following public policies would you prefer, with any modifications that you want to suggest?
    (a) No government intervention—the keen competition in the industry and public awareness of electricity costs can be counted on to provide economically efficient refrigerators. (The better insulated polyurethane models are already becoming more common.)
    (b) A labelling requirement specifying the annual usage of kilowatt-hours under average climatic and use conditions so that consumers could make more informed judgments.
    (c) Compulsory product standard limiting energy usage. Specify whether you prefer a modest limit such as 2000 kilowatt-hours, which could force Americans to smaller units such as the ones they made do with in 1960 (though larger than those that Europeans use now).

3. (For those who have worked with PV tables): Compute the marginal efficiencies of capital (rates of return) on the $34 incremental investment in model A and the $56 additional increment in model B. Use electricity prices of $.03 and $.06 per kilowatt-hour.

74

PROBLEM 33

SHOULD SMITH GIVE TO PRINCETON?

In the early 1950s, annual corporate gifts to education were approximately $100,000,000. Corporations with assets below $1,000,000 averaged 1.63 percent of net taxable income for all charitable gifts while larger corporations averaged 0.7 percent. New Jersey and many other states had passed laws permitting such institutions to make specified charitable donations of no more than 1 percent annually of stockholder equity. Federal law permitted income tax deductions up to 5 percent of corporate income for such charitable purposes.

In 1951, the board of directors of the A. P. Smith Manufacturing Company, a manufacturer of valves, fire hydrants, and related equipment, appropriated $1,500 as a gift to Princeton University. This was among the first gifts after the passing of a 1950 New Jersey law that supplemented earlier legislation in specifically listing colleges as among those institutions to which corporations could give money. Certain stockholders challenged the gift, and the company sought a court declaration that its board was acting within its powers.

The Stockholders' Case

The counsel for the stockholders argued that, while New Jersey legislation expressed public policy favorable to such contributions, it was unconstitutional on the ground of impairing the obligation of contracts. He asserted the following:

No case has been cited, and we have found none, which even indicated that under the reserved power or under the police power directors may be authorized to divert moneys, in which only the stockholders have an interest, for any purpose other than the advancement of the corporate objects. Neither the great work done by privately supported institutions of learning in this Country nor the difficulty which such institutions are now encountering in financing their operations affords any support to legislation which authorized fiduciaries to violate the terms of the instrument which fixes their power.

The presiding judge summed up the argument as follows:

The stockholders, who object to the aforementioned resolution passed by the company's directors, contend that the $1,500 contribution to Princeton, granted though not yet paid, is *ultra vires,* since there is no power in the charter of the company to make such contribution as the resolution calls for. They argue that the company may not use any of its corporate funds except in furtherance of its business needs, and only for the purpose of creating profit for its stockholders. They take the further position that since the corporation's charter constitutes a tri-partite contract, one between the State and the company, between the company and its stockholders, and, lastly, between the stockholders *inter se,* it is not within the power of the Legislature to alter or impair that contract by the enabling or permissive legislation consisting of the 1930 and 1950 acts, above mentioned.

The Corporation's Witnesses

The corporation presented in court an imposing list of witnesses, including distinguished business and educational leaders. Mr. Hubert F. O'Brien, the president of the company, testified that he considered the contribution to be a sound investment, that the public expects corporations to aid philanthropic and benevolent institutions, that they obtain good will in the community by doing so, and that their charitable donations create favorable environment

---

*This case is found in 13 N.J. 145, 98A. 2d 481 (1953), affirming in the New Jersey Supreme Court the holding of the lower court, found in 26 N.J. Super. 106, 97A. 2d 186 (1953).

for their business operations. He expressed the belief that in contributing to liberal-arts institutions, corporations were furthering their self-interest in assuring the free flow of properly trained personnel for administrative and other corporate employment. Frank W. Abrams, chairman of the board of the Standard Oil Company of New Jersey, testified that corporations are expected to acknowledge their public responsibilities in support of the essential elements of our free enterprise system. He indicated that it was not "good business" to disappoint "this reasonable and justified public expectation," nor was it good business for corporations "to take substantial benefits from their membership in the economic community while avoiding the normally accepted obligations of citizenship in the social community."

Dr. Harold W. Dodds, President of Princeton University, pointed to the civic welfare tasks performed by Princeton and other universities. He suggested that, "Unless funds are secured from business alumni, and other friends of education, then money may have to come from the Federal Government." Any replacement by governmental institutions would vastly change our society. "Democratic society will not long endure if it does not nourish within itself strong centers of nongovernmental fountains of knowledge, opinions of all sorts not governmentally or politically originated. If the time comes when all these centers are absorbed into government, then freedom as we know it, I submit, is at an end."

Court Decision

It is settled law here and in England that a corporation or association possesses not only those powers which are expressly conferred upon it by its charter, franchise or articles of association, but also all incidental powers reasonably designed or required to give fuller or greater effect to the expressed powers. An expressed power to a company to sell its wares does not require that with it there be also expressed the right to advertise its merchandise by the public press, radio, television, or any of the infinite variety of media of publicity and promotion. Such activity is a power present by necessary implication. So in respect of good will. Anything that tends to promote with the public a company's good will is a reasonable measure towards the corporate objective of earning profits.

There is also the broader question here involved, namely, that the contribution here in question is towards a cause which is intimately tied into the preservation of American business and the American way of life. Such giving may be called an incidental power, but when it is considered in its essential character, it may well be regarded as a major, though unwritten, corporate power. It is even more than that. In the court's view of the case it amounts to a solemn duty. . . .

It is to the credit and the glory of the common law that it has always had within itself the seed of change, keeping pace with the march of the years and the advance of thought。

Exactly 70 years ago the English Court of Chancery said, "Charity has no business to sit at boards of directors." Fifty years went by, with all the changes in industry that took place in that period, and the same court gave its judicial stamp of approval to a contribution of 100,000 pounds voted by a chemical company to several English universities for the "furtherance of scientific education and research."

Is the Corporation's Action Unconstitutional?

The constitutional objections raised by the defendants under both Federal and State Constitutions are substantially alike. So considered they amount to the claim that the legislation here in question impairs the obligation of contracts, deprives the defendants of property without due process, and, finally, constitutes a taking of private property for public purposes but without compensation. I do not regard those objections as tenable. The granting of the charter by the State to the plaintiff company has at all times been subject to the reserved power of the State to alter, suspend or repeal the same, in the discretion of the Legislature. . . . .

Even if it were assumed that the diversion of a corporate sum within the limits of the statutes does in some mathematical measure impair the rights of stockholders, it is not a *substantial* impairment.

The Court issued a declaratory judgment stating that the contribution was within the powers of the corporation and was upheld by the New Jersey Supreme Court in 1953.

Questions

1. With which of the hypotheses in this chapter is the behavior of A. P. Smith and other corporate givers consistent? Consider particularly the hypothesis of separation of ownership from control, the hypothesis of satisficing, and the hypothesis of long-run profit maximization.

2. Does the considerable attention to "public responsibilities" as stressed by Frank Abrams necessarily mean that simple profit-maximizing hypotheses are irrelevant for the analysis of all of a firm's decisions?

3. Do you agree that there is a special case for corporate giving to educational institutions, which, in the words of the judge, amounts to a "solemn duty"?

THE DISTRIBUTION OF INCOME

PROBLEM 34

LORENZ CURVES AND INCOME DISTRIBUTIONS

The Lorenz curve is a graphical presentation permitting the comparison of income distributions. The vertical axis represents the cumulative percentage of total national income; the horizontal axis, the percentage of the population (here expressed as families) cumulated from the lowest to the highest income. Exact equality of income would be represented by the straight diagonal line running from the lower left (20 percent of the families would receive 20 percent of the income; 50 percent of the families, 50 percent of the income, etc.). The departure of the Lorenz curve from the diagonal is a measure of the inequality of income.

The first column represents shares of before-tax income per family and includes money transfer payments as well as factor incomes; the third column is the hypothetical distribution of a country with no poverty, no upper-middle class, and a small but wealthy elite.

	(1) Income Share U.S., 1972 (percent)	(2) Cumulative Percent of Income	(3) Hypothetical Share of Income (percent)	(4) Cumulative Percent of Income
Lowest fifth (under $5,612)	5.4	_____	10.0	_____
Second fifth ($5,612-$9,299)	11.9	_____	12.0	_____
Middle fifth ($9,300-$12,854)	17.5	_____	14.0	_____
Fourth fifth ($12,855-$17,759)	23.9	_____	16.0	_____
Highest fifth ($17,760 and over)	41.4	_____	48.0	_____
(80-95 percent)	(25.5)	_____	(18.0)	_____
(95-100 percent) ($27,837 and over)	(15.9)	_____	(30.0)	_____

1. (a) Graph these distributions as Lorenz curves.

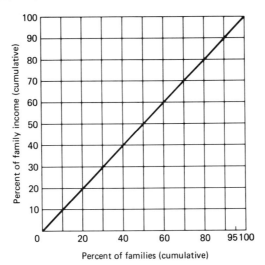

(b) Which family income distribution—United States, 1972, or the hypothetical one—most closely approaches absolute equality of income? Explain.

2. Imagine the distribution of income that might characterize a wholly middle-class society in which no significant group of families had an income below 75 percent of the average (about the amount the Bureau of Labor Statistics uses as a guide for a modest but comfortable standard of living) and no significant group had more than double the average income. Plot this distribution as a Lorenz curve; using the graph (i.e., comparing the areas between the Lorenz curves and the diagonal of income equality), estimate how much of a movement toward equality of income this would be from the 1972 distribution.

	Share of Income (percent)	Cumulative Percent of Income
Lowest fifth	_____	_____
Second fifth	_____	_____
Middle fifth	_____	_____
Fourth fifth	_____	_____
Highest fifth	_____	_____
(80-95 percent)	_____	_____
(Highest 5 percent)	_____	_____

3. Which of these three income distributions do you prefer? On what grounds?

4. The 1947 figures showed the following shares by fifths: 5.1, 11.8, 16.7, 23.2, and 43.3 (17.5 for the top 5 percent). Do you note any change in the equality of income distribution between 1947 and 1972?

PROBLEM 35

TWO CASES ON MINIMUM WAGES

A. *The Case of the Rural Mill Owner*

A traditional argument was that unionization (and/or a legal minimum wage) was necessary to prevent exploitation of labor by the monopsonistic firm—the only employer in an area, a fairly common situation. Not only would wages be raised, it was contended, but also employment would be *increased*.

Take the hypothetical case of Mr. Alfred Newman, whose mill was the only major employer in a rural county. Everyone available locally was on his payroll at the profit-maximizing wage ($1.20 per hour). He had decided not to expand output because he would have had to offer higher wages to attract workers from the next county. Then the United Textile Workers won a representation election and negotiated $1.50 as the minimum wage in the mill.

Questions

1. Show on the diagram what happens to the supply curve of labor with the new minimum wage.

2. What happens to the marginal-cost-of-labor (MLC) curve?

3. Where does the new MLC curve intersect the D curve for labor?

4. If Mr. Newman now wishes to maximize profits, how many people will he employ? _____

5. Assume that the union gets a further raise; at what level will it reduce employment below the original level? _____

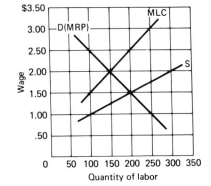

B. *The Case of the Unemployed Teen-ager*

Congress has just acted to increase unemployment. It did so by raising the legal minimum wage rate from $1.25 to $1.60 an hour, effective in 1968, and extending its coverage.

. . .

Women, teen-agers, Negroes and particularly Negro teen-agers will be especially hard hit. . . . The shockingly high rate of unemployment among teen-age Negro boys is largely a result of the present Federal minimum-wage rate. . . . Before 1956 unemployment among Negro boys aged 14 to 19 was around 8 to 11 percent, about the same as among white boys. Within two years after the legal minimum wages was raised from 75 cents to $1 an hour in 1956, unemployment among Negro boys shot up to 24 percent and among white boys to 14 percent. . . .*

---

*From Milton Friedman, "Minimum-Wage Rates," *Newsweek*, September 26, 1966.

The following table shows unemployment rates (in percent) for specific groups in recent years.

Year	Minimum Wage[a]	Overall Unemployment Rate	White Male	Nonwhite Male	White, 14-19 Years	Nonwhite, 14-19 Years
1961	$1.00	6.1%	5.1%	11.7%	15.3%	27.6%
1965	1.25	4.5	2.9	6.0	13.4	26.2
1966	1.40	3.8	22.2	4.9	11.2	25.4
1967	1.40	3.8	2.1	4.3	11.0	26.4

[a]These minimums do not apply universally. A number of occupations, such as agriculture and hospitals, are covered by lower minimums at present and did not reach $1.60 until 1971. States have minimum-wage laws to supplement federal coverage. Average hourly earnings in manufacturing were: 1956, $1.95; 1961, $2.32; 1965, $2.61; 1966, $2.72; 1967, $2.38; 1968, $3.01.
Source: Economic Report of the President, 1968.

In 1971 with overall unemployment slightly less than 6%, "the nonwhite teenage employment rate has risen to over 30%, more than twice that for whites." *(Monthly Economic Letter,* First National City Bank, December, 1971, p. 9.)

Questions

1. Would you say these figures tended to uphold Professor Friedman's hypothesis?

2. According to marginal-productivity theory, why would teen-agers especially be affected adversely by minimum-wage laws? Which teen-agers would gain from them?

3. In 1971, the AFL-CIO was strongly pressing for a $2 minimum wage and expanded occupational coverage. It vigorously opposed an amendment that would set the minimum for teen-agers at $1.25, and another that would hold it at $1.60.

    A former member of the Council of Economic Advisers, James Tobin, wrote: "People who lack the capacity to earn a decent living should be helped but they will not be helped by minimum-wage laws, trade union pressures or other devices which seek to compel employers to pay more than their work is worth. The likely outcome of such regulations is that the intended beneficiaries are not employed at all." *(Monthly Economic Letter,* First National City Bank, December, 1971, p. 10.) Consider pros and cons for the higher minimum and the amendment.

4. A new minimum wage of $2.00 was passed in 1974, despite the continued opposition of Prof. Friedman. A $2.10 minimum was slated for January 1, 1975, and $2.30 for 1976; coverage was extended, including private household workers. Do the ratios of average to minimum wages suggest that this new minimum is somewhat responsive to the Friedman and Tobin criticisms, given these average wages for private nonagricultural employment? Minimum wage at the time is in parentheses: 1956, $1.80 ($1.00); 1961, $2.14 ($1.25); 1966, $2.45 ($1.40); 1968, $2.85 ($1.60); 1974, $4.05 ($2.00).

PROBLEM 36

THE CHANCE OF BEING A POOR CHILD

You may already have noted the apparent paradox that, although the majority of the poor in the United States are white, the percentage of black families that are poor is much greater. The explanation, of course, is that there are many more white families. In analyzing the family status of poor children, three characteristics are particularly significant: race, sex of the head of household, and number of children.

The following table gives both the percentage of poor children and the percentage of total children for each of the family categories listed. The figures are for 1967 and the poverty level used was an income of $3,900 for a nonfarm family of four, with a lower level used for a farm family or a smaller family and a higher level used for a larger family. Despite the protests of Women's Lib, the Bureau of the Census considers an able-bodied male adult, if present, head of the family. The total number of children was estimated at 70,712,000 and the number of children in poverty at 10,648,000 or 15.1 percent of all children.

Percentage of Children in Poverty and Percentage of Total Children
(by family size and head of family)[a]

| Race and Sex of Family Head | Number of Children in Family | | | Total All |
	1-2	3-4	5 or More	Family Sizes
Nonwhite male	3.1 (2.7)	5.5 (3.2)	11.8 (4.1)	20.4 (10.0)
White male	8.3 (31.0)	14.6 (33.0)	17.9 (15.0)	40.8 (79.0)
Total male	11.4 (33.7)	20.1 (36.2)	29.7 (19.1)	61.2 (89.0)
Nonwhite female	3.6 (1.1)	7.1 (1.5)	10.0 (1.9)	20.7 (4.5)
White female	5.6 (3.0)	6.9 (2.3)	5.5 (1.2)	18.0 (6.5)
Total female	9.2 (4.1)	14.0 (4.8)	15.5 (4.1)	38.7 (13.0)
Total nonwhite	6.7 (3.8)	12.6 (4.7)	21.8 (6.0)	41.1 (14.5)
Total white	13.9 (34.0)	21.5 (35.3)	23.4 (16.2)	58.8 (85.5)
Total	20.6 (37.8)	34.1 (40.0)	45.2 (22.2)	99.9 (100.0)

[a]Percentages of children in poverty are given first, percentages of total children are in parentheses.

Questions

1. The majority of children in poverty are in:
   (a) (white/nonwhite) families
   (b) families with (four or fewer/more than four) children
   (c) families with (male/female) heads

2. Estimate by filling in the table below the relative chance of being poor for a person who is a member of a particular type of family. Divide (rounding off, approximating) the percentage of children in poverty by the percentage of total children to get a number that expresses the relative chance a child in each category has of being poor. The first and last rows are filled in for you to show the approximation desired. (For instance, a figure of 2 means twice the likelihood of being in poverty than that of the average child.)

Race and Sex of	Number of Children in Family			
Family Head	1-2	3-4	5 or More	Total
Nonwhite male	1+	2-	3-	2+
White male				
Total male				
Nonwhite female				
White female				
Total female				
Total nonwhite				
Total white				
Total	1/2+	3/4+	2+	1

3. Each of the figures in the table can be multiplied by 0.15 (15 percent of total children were in poverty in 1967) to estimate the probability of children of that category being in poverty.

    (a) For which categories were over 40 percent of the children in poverty?

    (b) For which categories were less than 10 percent in poverty?

4. (a) What do you conclude about the effects of race, sex of family head, and size of family on the proportion of children in poverty?

    (b) Does any of these characteristics individually account for the majority of children in poverty? Do the three characteristics collectively account for such a majority?

PROBLEM 37

POSITIVE THINKING ABOUT A
NEGATIVE INCOME TAX

The negative income tax plan cited in the text is closely similar to the Nixon Administration proposal and several congressional modifications of it that were being considered in 1971. Proponents estimated that it would add relatively little to government expenditures because (a) to a large extent, it would replace existing welfare programs with benefits at about the same level; (b) its guaranteed family income of $2,400 was well below the poverty level; (c) the marginal tax rate of 50 percent was far higher than that of the ordinary income tax, and together with the $2,400 minimum would eliminate benefits at the $4,800 level; and (d) it was available only on the condition that employable heads of families accepted available suitable employment.

A multimillion-dollar experiment was conducted in New Jersey and Pennsylvania, where seven variants of the negative income tax were tried. The income guarantee was varied from 50 to 100 percent of the poverty line ($3,300 for a family of four in 1968). The marginal rates of taxation—that is, reductions of benefits with earnings—ranged from 30 to 70 percent of earnings. The basic question to be answered concerned the incentive effect of such a program on male-headed families. (As a program official put it, "Stated in its baldest terms, many people fear that able-bodied men would simply quit work and live on the dole.") Therefore, all the plans and the control group included only such families.

Preliminary results reported in May, 1971, found statistically insignificant differences in earning changes between the control group and those in the various plans. The interpretation as reported in the *New York Times* of May 9, 1971, was more cautious. "There is still no indication of a precipitous withdrawal from the labor force by families who receive income maintenance payments. It appears that an income assistance program may give poor people, particularly the working poor, the ability to seek out better jobs." At the American Economic Association meetings in December, 1973, Professors Watts and Cain of the University of Wisconsin presented a more complete analysis. They found an insignificant change in the hours worked by men under the plan. While women worked less than before the plan, the absolute decline in hours was small because of low participation rates and few hours worked by women in these income classes.

None of the proposals given legislative consideration to date would do *all* of the following:

1. Fully incorporate the administration and rates of the negative income tax with the current U.S. income-tax structure.
2. Provide unconditionally an income that is at or above the poverty line.
3. Keep the marginal rate of taxation significantly below 50 percent in order to maintain earning incentives.
4. Make more progressive the income-tax structure for the $5,000-$50,000 income range.

What are some of the implications of the following Forbush proposal, which would accomplish these ends?

Each individual 18 years and older would receive a negative tax of $1,250 per year (this is a composite of the personal exemption of $750 and half of the standard deduction of $1,000). The first two dependents below 18 years would receive $750, the third $500, and subsequent dependents $300. (This reflects the present personal exemption, some allowance for economies of scale in child rearing, and the avoidance of economic incentives for large families.) There would be no other deductions from income such as the present charitable contributions, state and local taxes, interest paid, medical expenses, oil depletion, state and municipal bond interest, and so on. (Actually, the revenues raised could permit some deductions as a political expedient—Americans love their deductions.)

The tax structure could be extremely simple: 40 percent on income (other than the negative tax) from 0 to $20,000; 50 percent, from $20,000 to $50,000; and 60 percent, for income above

$50,000. (These rates seem less progressive than the 15 to 70 percent shown in Table 25-2 in the existing income-tax structure, but remember that a family of four will be offsetting the positive tax with the negative income tax of $4,000 and that few now pay the 70-percent rate because of the many opportunities for tax avoidance.)

One test that the negative income tax must pass is that of fiscal feasibility. The following rough check indicates that this proposal would have been more than adequate as a revenue raiser in 1970.

1. Positive tax liabilities
    40 percent of personal income less net transfers $300 billion
    Additional yield from 50- and 60-percent rates   20 billion
                                                                    320
2. Negative tax payments
    $1,250 x 133 million people 18 and over $167 billion
       600 (est. avg.) x 72 million under 18   43 billion
                                                                    210
3. Positive tax liabilities minus negative tax payments $110 billion
4. Adjustments
    Subtract personal contributions to social security $ 28 billion
    Add savings from elimination of 60 percent of govern-   46 billion
       ment transfer payments (some social security,
       veterans benefits, etc., are assumed to continue)
5. Net raised or saved by N.I.T. proposal $128 billion

Because this total substantially exceeds the $94 billion raised by the personal income tax, considerable fiscal leeway is left to cover loss of earned income by work dropouts and/or modification of this or other taxes—for example, the partial reintroduction of such popular deductions as charitable contributions, taxes paid to states and localities, and so forth.

Clearly the specific figures for taxes, benefits, and other government expenditures have been been vastly altered by inflation, 30 percent by 1974 and more when you are considering the problem. But the implications and pros and cons will be much the same.

Questions

1. In each of the following versions of the New Jersey negative income tax experiment, calculate the marginal rate of taxation:
       (a) A family of four receives a negative tax of $3,300 with zero earnings, and nothing with earnings of $6,600. _____

       (b) A man earning $100 a week with a family of six is given $28.50 negative tax a week; if his income drops to zero, he will receive $58.50. _____

       (c) A man with a family of five and $96 a week income receives $10.75 a week; if his earnings fall to $50, he will receive $43 a week; and if he earns nothing, he will receive $78 a week. _____

2. Complete the following table, including the two columns in the center, which give the proportion of before-tax income paid (or received in negative taxes). Figure the Forbush tax first. Is this negative income tax proposal more progressive than the present tax structure?

Family of 4, Before-tax Income	1970 Tax			Forbush Negative Income-tax Proposal		
	Tax[a]	After-tax Income	Tax ÷ Income[b]	Tax ÷ Income[b]	Tax	After-tax Income
$ 0	$ 0	$ 0	0	—	$ -4,000	$ 4,000
2,000	0	2,000		-1.600		
4,000	60	3,940	.015			
7,000	590	6,410				
10,000	1,090	8,910		0	0	10,000
12,000	1,550	10,450				
20,000	3,110	16,990		.200	4,000	16,000
30,000	5,800	24,200				
40,000	9,900	30,100				
50,000	13,300	36,700			19,000	31,000
100,000	37,600	62,400				
1,000,000	600,000	400,000			588,000	412,000

[a]This assumes a 10-percent itemized deduction list for incomes over $10,000. Many in the higher brackets had greater deductions as well as exempt income and thus paid less, so increased impact of negative tax proposal on upper-middle and high incomes is understated.
[b]Before-tax income.

3.   Consider the implications of the negative income-tax proposal as part of the ordinary income tax. Would you favor or oppose it? What modifications would you see as desirable?

NATIONAL INCOME ACCOUNTS; DEBT AGGREGATES

PROBLEM 38

INCOME AGGREGATES AND PRICE DEFLATORS

1. From the figures given, calculate the 1929 GNP in 1958 dollars and the implicit price deflator that converts current 1973 GNP to constant 1958 dollars.

	GNP, 1958 Dollars (billions)	GNP, current Dollars (billions)	Implicit Price Deflator
1929	_____	103.1	50.6
1958	447.3	447.3	100.0
1973	839.2	1294.9	_____

(a) What was the percentage increase in current dollar GNP between 1929 and 1973?

_____

(b) What was the percentage increase in the prive level, as measured by the implicit price deflator, between 1929 and 1973? _____

(c) What was the percentage increase in *real* GNP between 1929 and 1973? _____

2. Disposable income in the United States rose from $83 billion in 1929 to $882 billion in 1973, or by more than 10 times. Per capita disposable income in constant 1958 dollars rose from $1,145 to $2,890, by about 2½ times. The population rose from 121 million to 210 million, or by just about 75 percent.
(a) What happened to the consumer price level: (fell/stayed the same/increased 2½ times/ up 9 times/no way of telling)?
(b) GNP increased by an even greater ratio than disposable income from 1929 to 1973. Why?

PROBLEM 39

FROM CORPORATE STATEMENTS TO NATIONAL INCOME

For 1967, the U.S. Steel Corporation reports its income as follows (figures given in millions):

Products and services sold	$4,067
Costs (applicable to goods sold)	
Employment costs, including benefits	$1,872
Products and services bought	1,432
Wear and exhaustion of facilities	355
Interest and other costs on long-term debt	54
State, local, and miscellaneous taxes	106
Estimated federal tax on income	76
	$3,895
Income	$ 172
Dividends declared	130
Income reinvested in business	$ 42

In addition, U.S. Steel's semifinished and finished product inventories increased by $70 million (assume that 40 percent of this increase represented purchased components and 60 percent was factor payments).

Questions

1. Estimate the value added in production by U.S. Steel in 1967 by using the definition of value of production minus purchases from other firms. (For this question, include depreciation and state and local taxes as purchases from other firms.)

2. Show that the factor payments by U.S. Steel to income recipients is equal to this total:

Employee compensation	_____
Interest	_____
Income before income taxes	_____
Factor payments in producing inventory increase	_____
Total	_____

3. In 1973 U.S. Steel's sales of products and services had increased to $7,045 million, or by 73 percent. Would the value added by production necessarily have risen by 73 percent? Why or why not?

PROBLEM 40

HOW THE NATIONAL ECONOMIC
BUDGET GETS ITS NUMBERS

A widely used format that shows the equality of the receipts and expenditures approaches to the GNP has been called the *national economic budget*. It has proved particularly useful in forecasting because it breaks receipts and expenditures into four major sectors, allowing comparison and the striking of a balance for each sector. The figures you are initially given in the table add up to national income on the receipts side and to GNP on the expenditures side. The additional information will allow you to balance receipts and expenditures, to break expenditures down into further categories of economic significance, and to adjust for intersector payments. Whether a particular bit of added data is entered once or twice is indicated in the parentheses following the figures. A few technical adjustments have already been made, and the headings will guide your work. There are three points you might note as you go along:

1. Imports are subtracted from exports because the national-income accounts do not adjust expenditures for their import component.
2. Consumer interest is both added and subtracted in the Persons account. It is added because national income includes only income from productive services; it is subtracted from disposable income because, while an expenditure, it is not included in consumption, which would make it a part of national production. The point of this practice, which was introduced only a few years ago, was to avoid having GNP go up simply because consumers were deeper in hock. (Interest on the federal debt had long been treated as a transfer rather than a payment for productive services.) This is an illustration of how national-income accounting conventions have led to interesting philosophical debates and different answers.
3. All figures are given in billions of dollars rounded off to strike proper balances and are the preliminary estimates for 1973. (You will find differences in later data for either of these two reasons. An early revision was to $1294.9 billion.)

Additional information (number of entries)

Increase in inventories	7	(1)	Residential construction	58	(1)
Federal nondefense expenditures	33	(1)	Plant and equipment expenditure	136	(1)
Consumer expenditures on non-durable goods	336	(1)	Indirect business taxes (and minor adjustments)	117	(1)
Consumer expenditures on durable goods	131	(1)	Personal transfers to foreigners	1	(2)
Consumer expenditures on services	338	(1)	Government transfers to foreigners	2	(2)
			Personal income taxes	153	(2)
Contributions for social insurance	92	(2)	Corporate income taxes	56	(2)
Interest paid by federal government	16	(1)	Defense expenditures	74	(1)
Consumer interest paid	23	(1)	State and local government expenditures	170	(1)
Dividends	28	(2)	Additions to personal income for business transfers, government, and consumer interest	43	(1)
Capital consumption allowances	110	(1)			
Transfer payments to persons	112	(2)			

91

National Economic Budget: Receipts and Expenditures by Major Economic Groups

Group	Receipts (+)		Expenditures on Goods and Services (-)		Balance (receipts - expenditures)
Persons or households	Wages and other compensation of employees	785		_____	
	Income of proprietors	84		_____	
	Rental income of persons	25		_____	
	Net interest to persons	51			
	+ _____ (-) _____				
	+ _____ (-) _____				
	+ _____				
	Disposable personal income _____				
	Less: consumer interest _____				
	transfer payments				
	to foreigners _____				
	Adjusted DPI _____		Consumption	805	54
Business (including investment)	Capital consumption allowances _____			_____	
	Corporate profits less inventory valuation adjustment	109		_____	
	(-) _____			_____	
	(-) _____		Gross private		
	Gross retained earnings of business _____		domestic investment	201	-66
International	Transfer payments to foreigners				
	from persons _____				
	from government _____		Exports -		
	Total transfers _____		Imports	5	- 2
Government	Taxes: Transfers:			_____	
	(+) _____ (-) _____			_____	
	(+) _____ (-) _____		Government pur-	_____	
	(+) _____ (-) _____		chases of		
	(+) _____		goods and		
	Net. rec. (taxes - transfers) _____		services	277	11
Statistical discrepancy		3			+ 3
Totals (GNP)	_____			1288	0

92

PROBLEM 41

THE PARADOX OF DEBT

On few issues are people more ambivalent than on the virtues and evils of debt. The traditional advice as given by Shakespeare, "Neither a borrower nor a lender be," and Ben Franklin, "Who goeth a borrowing goeth a sorrowing," has been firmly against it. The opposing position has been well expressed by the admonition of the anonymous capitalist to the young man, "If you wish to become rich, borrow," and by Artemus Ward, "Let us all be happy and live within our means, even if we have to borrow money to do it."

One way to see the national debt in perspective is to compare it not only with the GNP, but also with other types of debt. The table below summarizes debt of several types for selected years from "Net Public and Private Debt," as published in the annual *Economic Report of the President,* 1974. It does not include the debt of financial institutions (deposits, life insurance reserves), or the totals would be about 50 percent higher. Remember that every debt is an asset to someone else, so the consumer sector is a very large net creditor, and the business and government sectors are the net debtors. (In the table, all figures are in billions of current dollars.)

Year	GNP	Total Debt	Federal Debt[a]	State and Local	Total Corporate	Total Individual	Nonfarm Mortgage[b]	Consumer Credit[b]
1929	$ 103.1	$ 191.9	$ 16.5	$ 13.6	$ 88.9	$ 72.9	$ (31.2)	$ (7.1)
1933	55.6	168.5	24.3	16.3	76.9	51.0	(26.3)	(3.9)
1940	99.7	189.8	44.8	16.4	75.6	53.0	(26.1)	(8.3)
1945	211.9	405.9	252.5	13.4	85.3	54.7	(27.0)	(5.7)
1950	284.8	486.2	218.1	21.7	142.1	104.3	(54.8)	(21.5)
1960	503.7	874.2	243.3	64.9	302.8	263.3	(151.3)	(56.1)
1965	683.9	1,243.6	275.3	98.3	454.3	415.7	(236.8)	(89.9)
1970	977.1	1,854.1	339.9	144.8	793.5	575.9	(320.9)	(127.2)
1973	1,294.9	2,525.8	408.9	184.5	1,111.1	821.3	(480.1)	(180.5)

[a]Includes federal financing agency debt which totaled 59.8 in 1973.
[b]Included in total individual debt as indicated by parentheses.

Questions

1. The growth of the total debt since 1929 seems enormous. Compute the ratios of the debt to GNP for the dates below:

Year	Total Debt/GNP
1929	_____
1933	_____
1945	_____
1960	_____
1970	_____
1973	_____

(a) Does this give you a different perspective?

(b) For what year does the ratio seem extraordinarily high? _____ What does this suggest about the type of economic event that would make the level of debt unusually burdensome?

(c) About two-thirds of the debt is long term (over one year). Do rising prices help reduce the burden of this component of the debt? Explain briefly.

2. Compute roughly the ratios of the different types of debt, comparing 1973 with 1929 and 1945:

	Ratio to 1929	Ratio to 1945
GNP	13–	6
Total debt	12	6+
Federal	_____	_____
State and local	_____	_____
Corporate	_____	_____
Total invididual	_____	_____
Mortgage	_____	_____
Consumer	_____	_____

(a) Which have risen by *substantially* more than the GNP since 1929? (Use ratio of 1969 GNP to 1929 GNP for comparison.)

(b) Which have risen by *substantially* more than the GNP since 1945?

(c) How do you explain this difference in the two periods?

3. What seems to be the major reason for the increase in the federal debt in the past?

4. Discussion has focused on the impact of federal deficits or surpluses. Some economists suggest that more attention must be paid to the fiscal policies of states and localities. What evidence is there in this table to support this contention?

5. Some have viewed with alarm the rise in consumer credit (which is essentially short-term debt). Disposable personal income was $207 billion in 1950, $350 billion in 1960, and $883 billion in 1973. What tentative conclusion do you come to when you compare consumer credit with disposable personal income? (Consumer credit was $180.2 billion in 1973.)

NATIONAL INCOME ANALYSIS

PROBLEM 42

MULTIPLIERS AND WITHDRAWALS

The multiplier can be defined in terms of withdrawals from the circular flow, or specifically as the reciprocal of $\Delta W/\Delta Y$, that is: $\Delta Y/\Delta W$. Students sometimes have difficulty with the discrepancy between a multiplier of 10 that is indicated by a consumer's marginal propensity to save of .1 and that of about 2 which has been found to apply to many empirical studies of our complex economy. This problem seeks to show how the apparent multiplier of 10 is diminished to about 2 as the economic model takes on greater realism, with an increase in withdrawals related to income.

Economy A: Closed, Ungoverned, Without Business Savings

In this economy all income is disposable ($Y = Y_d$), and the only withdrawal is personal saving. Assuming that $.1Y_d$ is saved, then $S_p = .1Y_d = .1Y$. (Remember, $\Delta W/\Delta Y$ = the sum of the coefficients of Y in the various withdrawal functions.)
$\Delta W/\Delta Y = $ _____, and the multiplier is _____.

Economy B: Closed, Ungoverned, with Business Savings

In this economy it is assumed that firms do not distribute all of their income. Assume that business savings (S_b) = $.1Y$ and only $.9Y$ is disposable income to households. Then $S_p = .1Y_d = (.1)(.9Y) = .09Y$.
$\Delta W/\Delta Y = $ _____, and the multiplier is _____.

Economy C: Closed, Governed, with Business Savings

With government, another withdrawal in the form of taxes is introduced. It is conceivable that such taxes could be unrelated to Y, for example, head taxes so that $T = \$100$ billion. Would the multiplier be affected in this case? _____ Why?

It is more realistic to assume that taxes will be related to income and that the government will be concerned with transferring income to the old and the poor. With such transfers treated as negative taxes, assume $T_n = .3Y - 75$. Y_d now equals $Y - .1Y - .3Y + 75$, and $S_p = .1(.6Y + 75)$.
$\Delta W/\Delta Y = $ _____, and the multiplier is _____.

Economy D: Open, Governed, with Business Savings

With trade opened up to foreign countries, not all expenditures will be made domestically and thus in the economy's circular flow. Assume that imports (M) - $.04Y$ and that other withdrawals have the same relationship to Y as in economy C.
$\Delta W/\Delta Y = $ _____, and the multiplier is _____.

PROBLEM 43

THE DETERMINATION OF EQUILIBRIUM INCOME

A. *A Tabular and Graphic Approach*

The aggregate-demand schedule shows the various components of intended spending at each income level. Fill in the blanks in the table and plot the data on the graph. Assume imports and exports are zero throughout and that all government expenditures are on goods and services.

Level of GNP = Y (billions of dollars)	C	I	G	AD	J = I + G X	Y - C = W
0	90	10	40	140	50	-90
50	120	10	40			
100	150	10	40			
150	180	10	40			
200	210	10	40			
250	240	10	40			
300	270	10	40			
350	300	10	40			
400	330	10	40			
450	360	10	40			
500	390	10	40			

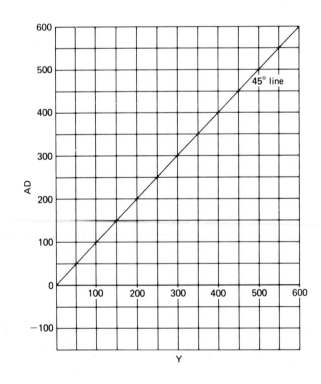

(a) GNP is at equilibrium level at _____ .
    At this level, AD = _____   W = _____
                    Y = _____   J = _____

(b) Write the equation for the consumption schedule, the AD schedule, and the W schedule.
    (Hint: These are linear equations of the form *a + by.)*

(c) The C and W equations added together should equal _____ .

B. *An Algebraic Approach*

The purpose of this problem is to work through algebraically the determination of equilibrium income for a simple economy smaller than but similar to that of the United States and then to work out a tabular and graphic presentation for an open, governed economy.

The households in this economy behave simply. They spend 90 percent of disposable income (Y_d) on consumption (one-thirtieth of this, or 3 percent of Y_d, goes for imports). The government (federal, state, and local) manages to collect 40 percent of GNP or Y in taxes. It purchases $200 billion of goods and services including $15 billion of purchases abroad, the latter largely related to defense and brush-fire wars. It also transfers $75 billion to persons for social security, welfare, veterans benefits, and the like; these can be treated as negative taxes, so *net* taxes are $T_n = .4Y - 75$ (billion dollars).

Gross private domestic investment is $125 billion, of which $5 billion is for foreign equipment and components. Much of the financing comes from gross business saving (capital consumption allowances and retained earnings) which amounts in total to 10 percent of GNP.

Exports are $40 billion, but $5 billion represents the materials and components that were initially purchased abroad.

Before striking a balance between J and W to see what the equilibrium GNP is, examine Y_d, which will determine consumption. Because business is keeping $.1Y$ and the government gets $.4Y$, the amount of income at the disposal of the consumer is $.5Y$ plus $75 billion of transfers received from government. Consumption therefore equals $.9(.5Y + 75)$ or $.45Y + 67.5$. Household savings would be equal to $Y_d - C$, or $.05Y + 7.5$.

Gross injections and withdrawals can now be equated to determine equilibrium GNP.

J	W
$I = 125$	$S = S_p + S_b = .05Y + 7.5 + .1Y = .15Y + 7.5$
$G = 200$	$T = .4Y - 75$
$X = 40$	$M = 25 + .03Y_d = 27.25 + .015Y$
365	$.565Y - 40.25$

Note that all injections are assumed to be autonomous and that all withdrawals are rising functions of GNP, as was the case in the text.

Finding equilibrium GNP is simply a matter of using the condition $J = W$ so that $.565Y = 405.25$. To save you long division, GNP = 717 and C = 390.

The same result could be obtained by using adjusted injections, which are more theoretically satisfying because an injection composed of a withdrawal (imported goods) is not going to influence GNP directly. Then we would have:

Injections	Withdrawals
$I^* = 120$	$S = .15Y + 7.5$
$G^* = 185$	$T = .4Y - 75$
$X^* = 35$	$M_c = 2.25 + .015Y$
340	$.565Y - 65.25$

Note that all imports have been netted out except for imported consumption goods. Setting adj J = adj W and simplifying, we have exactly what we had before: $.565Y = 405.25$. We should note that $C*$, the consumption of domestic goods which constitutes the ongoing circular flow, is equal to $390 - M_c$, or 377. (Calculate to see why.)

Only in the second of these cases does C or $C*$ added to J fulfill the condition of equaling AD or E, which has been defined as equal to GNP at equilibrium. For diagrammatic simplicity we would like this condition to be true as well as $J = W$. We also now can set AD = GNP(Y) and get the same results:

$$Y = E = AD = C* + J* = C* + I* + G* + X*[1]$$
$$Y = .45Y + 67.5 - 2.25 - .015Y + 340$$

which reduces to our old friend $.565Y = 405.25$.

Questions

1. First fill in the table below. The symbol headings have all been described in the material above. Then on the graph plot AD, $C*$, $J*$, and $W*$.

GNP	$J*$	S	T_n	M_c	$W*$	$C*$ $(C - M_c)$	AD $(C* + J*)$
0	340	8	− 75	2	− 65	65.5	405.5
200	340						
400	340						
600	340						
717	340	115	212	13	340	377.0	717.0
800	340						

2. At what level of GNP does AD intersect the 45° line of equality between AD and GNP?

3. What does the vertical distance between AD and $C*$ consist of? At equilibrium what other magnitude is also equal to this distance?

---

[1]The asterisks denote that the GNP components have been netted of imports. Since these magnitudes are not generally available, this equation can be written $Y = AD = C + I + G + X - M$ with the imports netted from the total. You can check to see that this equation is numerically equivalent.

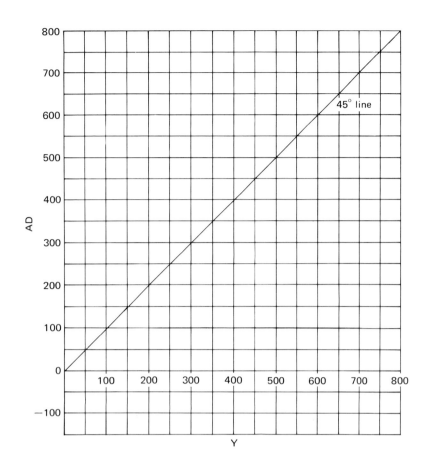

PROBLEM 44

SHOULD WE COUNT CARS AS CONSUMPTION?

Many forecasters treat most consumption outlays quite differently from automobile expenditures. Consumption outlays other than on automobiles are taken as a function of income only, whereas consumer expenditures on automobiles are treated as essentially autonomous, with income only one of a number of influencing factors such as size, age, and structure of existing automobile stocks, availability of consumer credit, and number of new households created. Do the following data indicate that such differential treatment, analogous with investment, may be justified?

Our starting point is a study of consumption data from 1946 to 1965 that has produced the equation $C_O = .884Y_d$, where C_O is personal outlays less automobiles and parts, and where personal outlays equal personal consumption expenditures plus personal transfer payments to foreigners and interest paid on consumer debt. This equation could obviously have stood improvement for the 1966-1973 period, but the premise still may hold that automobile purchases are not so close to a constant fraction of income as are other goods, and that in fact they are akin enough to saving and investment so that the combined total percentage of automobile purchases plus saving will vary less than savings alone.

Questions

1. Given the following data, how well was C_O predicted? Concentrate on the years 1966-1973. (Figures are given in billions of dollars.) Calculate answers for the blanks.

Year	Actual Y_d	C +	Interest and Transfers	Expenditures on Autos - and Parts	=	C_O	Predicted $C_O = .884Y_d$ *	Actual C_O/Y_d
1954	$257.4	$236.5	$ 4.6	$13.6		$227.5	227.5	0.884
1955	275.3	254.4	5.1	18.4		241.1	243.4	0.876
1960	350.0	325.2	7.8	20.1		312.9	309.4	0.894
1966	511.9	466.3	13.0	30.3		449.0	452.5	0.877
1967	546.3	492.1	13.9	30.5		474.6	473.6	0.869
1968	591.2	536.2	15.1	37.5		513.8	512.5	0.869
1969	634.4	579.5	16.7	40.2		556.0	550.0	0.876
1970	691.7	617.6	17.8	37.3		598.1	599.7	0.865
1971	746.0	667.2	18.7	46.6		639.1	648.8	0.857
1972	797.0	726.5	20.7	52.8		694.4	690.1	0.871
1973	903.7	805.2	24.2	57.9		——	——	——

*Source: Economic Report of the President, 1974. *.867Y_d from 1967-1973.*

2. (a) You should have noted that consumer outlays minus automobiles were relatively lower in the period 1967-1973; $.867Y_d$ instead of $.884Y_d$ proves to have been much closer. The validity of this forecasting method (excluding automobiles from the general consumption function) depends upon automobile purchases' and savings' being a fairly constant proportion of income, more constant than either of them separately. Check this hypothesis for the years 1966-1973 from the data below. The deviations from the average (mean) of the two series together should be less than the sum of the deviations of the two series separately or, more particularly, the deviations from automobile purchases plus savings in the third column should be less than those from savings alone.

100

	Auto Expenditures		Savings		$1 - C_o/Y_d$	
	$\div Y_d$	Deviation from Mean	$\div Y_d$	Deviation from Mean	$\div Y_d$	Deviation from Mean
1966	0.060	_____	0.064	_____	0.123[a]	_____
1967	0.056	_____	0.074	_____	0.131	_____
1968	0.063	_____	0.067	_____	0.131[a]	_____
1969	0.063	_____	0.060	_____	0.124[a]	_____
1970	0.054	_____	0.081	_____	0.135	_____
1971	0.062	_____	0.081	_____	0.143	_____
1972	0.068	_____	0.062	_____	0.129[a]	_____
1973	0.064	_____	0.082	_____	0.146	_____
Sum	0.490		0.571		1.062	
Mean	0.061 or 6.1%		0.071 or 7.1%		0.133 or 13.3%	
Sum of deviation[b]		_____		_____		_____

[a] Discrepancies of 0.001 are due to rounding.
[b] Disregard sign in adding deviations. For simplicity, mean has been rounded off.

(b) Why might the purchase of an automobile be more akin to savings and investment than to consumption?

Note that $Y_d - C_o$ equals auto expenditures plus savings, so that $1 - C_o/Y_d$ is the average propensity to buy autos and save. Briefly summarize your findings.

3. How big a percentage *change* in auto sales occurred in 1955 compared with 1954, as a fraction of the change in disposable income? _____ In 1967 compared with 1966? _____

Why do you think auto sales fluctuate more widely and more erratically in relationship to GNP than do expenditures on other goods? Keep in mind the fact that 1955 was a year of recovery, and that the term "minicession" (small recession) was coined for 1967.

4. (Optional.) Check to see if 1974 data (and subsequent years if available) are well predicted by $C_o = .867Y_d$, which fits the 1967-1972 period so well (one of mild inflation with a recession in 1970-1971).

THE "GNP GAP" AND INVESTMENT EXPENDITURES

The deflationary gap is the amount by which aggregate demand is smaller than the amount necessary to produce a full-employment equilibrium. The GNP gap differs from this in two respects:

1. It is the different between "potential," or full-employment, GNP and actual GNP. As indicated in the figure below, it is measured horizontally along the axis rather than vertically. (When, as in the figure at the end of the case, the horizontal axis is time, then the difference between potential and actual GNP is measured vertically.)
2. The actual GNP may differ from the equilibrium GNP.

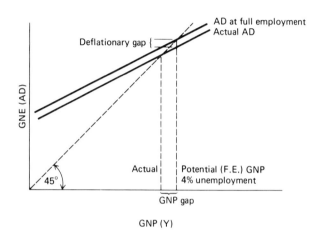

You are asked in this problem to investigate the relationship of changes in investment (as measured by gross private domestic investment expressed in constant 1958 dollars) and changes in the GNP gap. Because investment is an important injection, the hypothesis to be tested is that substantial year-to-year increases in investment will reduce the gap of potential minus actual GNP, whereas reductions will increase the gap.

First, examine the problem of measuring the gap, which is primarily a problem of measuring potential GNP. In its 1966 *Economic Report,* the Council of Economic Advisers (CEA) had the following to say:

> In the last four Economic Reports, the Council has discussed the concept of potential GNP, defined as the volume of goods and services that the economy would ordinarily produce at the interim target unemployment rate of 4 percent. The measurement of potential GNP must incorporate the effects of the higher productivity, the larger labor force, and the fuller work schedules which accompany reduced unemployment.
>
> Potential GNP does not stand still. Over time, population trends add to the number of persons in the labor force. Furthermore, increases in the quantity and quality of capital, advances in technology, and improvements in the quality of labor raise the potential productivity of the labor force.
>
> The evidence indicates that, from the mid-1950's and into the early 1960's, the potential labor force grew at the rate of about 1¼ percent a year. Normal growth of man-hour productivity for the entire work force (including Government as well as private workers) was 2½ percent a year. Hours worked a year trended downward at a rate of nearly one-fourth of 1 percent annually. Thus, potential GNP grew by 3½ percent a year.

103

For recent years, a real growth rate of actual GNP somewhat greater than 3½ percent has been required to hold the unemployment rate constant. Hence, the Council last year raised its estimated rate of growth of potential GNP to 3-3/4 percent, beginning in 1963. More rapid growth of the labor force will further increase the growth rate of potential GNP in the years ahead. . . .

The disparity or "gap" between potential and actual output . . . represents the goods and services foregone because of the underutilization of resources. The persistent gap since the mid-1950's has meant a total of $260 billion (in 1958 prices) in lost output.

In the *Economic Report of the President* for 1970, the CEA changed the calculations for future potential GNP. It stated:

Potential output is considered to be the output the economy would produce when operating at a 3.8 percent unemployment rate. This is slightly above the rate in the last half of 1969 when actual output was considered to be close to the potential. The annual growth of real potential output is determined by the growth of the labor force, estimated at 1-3/4 percent per year, and the growth of output per manhour. . . . The overall productivity rate (is estimated at) about 2.8 percent per year. Combined with the estimates of labor onput, this yields about a 4.3 percent rate of growth of potential real GNP.

The *Economic Report* for 1974 raised the question of "whether we were at 'potential' even though output was 2-3/4% below the commonly measured figure of 'potential' output." It suggested that a full-employment rate might be defined at 4.6 percent unemployment in 1973 to recognize the increasing proportion of women and youths in the work force, groups with traditionally higher unemployment rates. It noted that the work force had been rising by over 2 percent a year in 1972 and 1973 and hours worked per person had not declined, but that productivity was rising by less than predicted. This view that the potential as previously calculated could not have been a sensible goal in 1973 also reflected the material shortages and inflation of the times.

Questions

1. Calculate the annual change in the GNP gap and the annual change in investment and fill in the last two columns below (all GNP and GPDI figures are in billions of 1958 dollars). If you can get the figures, complete the table.

	(1) Potential GNP	(2) Actual GNP	(3) GNP Gap (1) − (2)	(4) Percent Unemployment	(5) GPDI	(6) Change in Gap	(7) Change in Investment
1955	$440	$438	$ 2	4.4	$ 75.4	−16.0[a]	+16.0
1956	455	446	9	4.2	74.3	+ 7.0	− .9
1957	471	452	19	4.3	68.8		
1958	487	447	40	6.8	60.9		
1959	504	476	28	5.5	73.6		
1960	521	488	33	5.6	72.4		
1961	539	497	42	6.7	69.0		
1962	558	530	28	5.6	79.4		
1963	579	551	28	5.7	82.5		
1964	601	581	20	5.2	87.8		
1965	623	617	6	4.6	99.2		
1966	647	658	−11	3.8	109.3		
1967	673	675	− 2	3.8	101.2	+ 9.0	− 8.1
1968	699	707	− 8	3.6	105.7		
1969	727	727	− 0	3.5	111.3		
1970	757	723	33	4.9	103.0		
1971	789	745	44	5.9	110.0		
1972	823	791	32	5.6	125.0		
1973	860	839	21	4.9	138.0		
1974	894	821	73	5.6	126.0	+52.0	−12.0
1975	930						
1976	967						

[a] Computed using 1954 data also, which are not given. Potential rises by 3.5 percent through 1962; 3.75 percent 1962–1965; 4 percent, 1966–1969; 4.3 percent, 1970–1973; 4 percent, 1974–1976.

Source: *Economic Report of the President,* 1974 and 1975.

2. Test the hypothesis that increases in investment are associated with reductions in the GNP gap and decreases with widening of the gap, by using the following breakdown.

Change in Real Investment	Changes in Gap in Associated Year (potential − actual GNP)	Average Change in Gap
Over +10		
+3 to +9		
0 to −6		
−7.5 and below		

3. What is your conclusion? Why would you expect this?

4. What other factors could influence the gap by their effects on actual GNP? Particularly note that the sum of real government purchases of goods and services and net exports declined in the following years (in billions of dollars): 1955, -3.5; 1959, -1.4; 1969, -2.6; 1970, -4.5; 1971, -2.8.

5. The rise in potential GNP is explained entirely in terms of potential labor input and labor productivity. How, then, does investment influence potential GNP?

6. Complete the two parts of the figure from the data in the previous table. Use annual rather than quarterly figures (and thus center in the space for the year).

Gross National Product, Actual and Potential, and Unemployment Rate

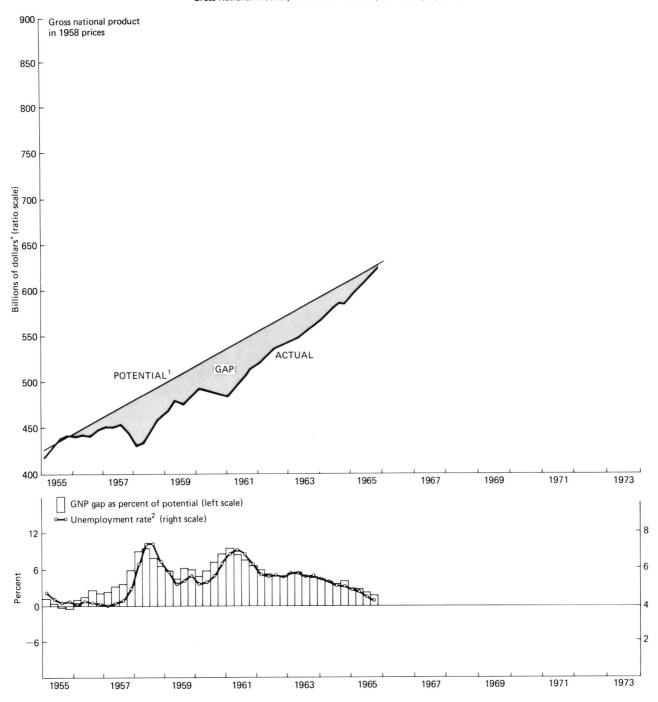

*Seasonally adjusted annual rates.
[1]Trend line of 3½ percent through middle of 1955 to 1962 IV; trend line of 3¼ percent thereafter.
[2]Unemployment as percent of civilian labor force, seasonally adjusted.
Sources: Department of Commerce, Department of Labor, and Council of Economic Advisers.

MONEY, BANKS, AND GNP

PROBLEM 46

DID THE SILVER MAKE THE QUARTER VALUABLE?

Before 1873 and after 1965, the silver bullion in a silver dollar was worth $1.00 or more. In between, it dropped to as low as $.22. In the late 1950s and 1960s, it became apparent that the rapidly increasing demand for silver both for coinage and industrial uses was increasing far more rapidly than the newly mined supplies (silver is largely a by-product of other mining). The world price was maintained first at $.906 and then at $1.293 an ounce, first through purchases of excess supplies and then through sales by the U.S. Treasury.

In 1963, the retirement of silver certificates was authorized. These were backed by 371¼ grains of silver bullion, the same as in a silver dollar. By 1968, this retirement was completed and the right to receive bullion for a silver certificate was repealed. For all practical purposes, silver coins had disappeared either into private hoards or into Treasury stocks by late 1968. The government had replaced them with nonsilver dimes and quarters and a half dollar of only 40 percent silver content.

Price of Silver and the Cost-of-Living Index in Selected Years

	Price per Ounce (cents)	Value of Silver in Silver Dollar (cents)	Cost-of-living Index (1957-1959 = 100)
1929	53	41	59.7
1932	25	22	47.6
1940[a]	71.1[a]	55[a]	48.8
	(35)	(27)	
1951-1961	90.6[a]	70	90.5-104.2
1965	129.3	100	109.9
1968 (approx. range)	190-235	147-178	121.5 (July)

[a]The 71.1-cent price was the U.S. government support price for newly mined domestic silver. The 35-cent price was the world market price. From 1951 to 1961, the world price corresponded approximately to the postwar government-support price.

Foresighted hoarders of silver certificates were able to get silver bullion before June 1968 at 129.3 cents an ounce and to sell it at higher prices. Any premiums received by silver coin holders would reflect anticipated scarcity values for collections, for illegal melting down of coins, or for speculation on the eventual legalization of the recovery of the silver from coins (which has now been done). For example, two New York businessmen who paid 10 percent over face value and melted down several thousand dollars of silver coins for sale at about $1.90 per ounce were arrested in December 1968 for these activities.

Questions

1. Did the fluctuations in the value of silver in coins and for backing silver certificates have any direct correspondence with the value of this money from 1929 to 1965?

2. What gave value to silver money in this period?

3. Comment on this quotation: "By 1965 silver became just too valuable to use as coins." In 1965, in those countries regularly reporting, industrial demand totaled 275 million ounces and was increasing by 5 percent per year. Reported world newly mined supply was 275 million ounces and not increasing at current prices, and corresponding coinage demand (mostly U.S.) was 300 million ounces a year.

4. By September, 1970, the price of silver had dropped to $1.50, but in the inflationary period of 1973 and 1974 the per-ounce price rose more than $2 to almost $6.
    (a) What was a likely reason for the price decline after the United States stopped coinage?

        (b) What was a likely reason for the abrupt price rise accompanying the sharp inflation of 1973 and 1974?

PROBLEM 47

IS IT TRUE WHAT THEY SAY ABOUT M AND GNP?

If the supply of money has a substantial effect on overall economic activity and prices, relationships should be perceived between the money supply and GNP. Particularly suggestive would be one in which changes in money preceded changes in GNP. This problem is designed to examine possible relationships. Below are some relevant data for recent years. MS_1 is the narrow money supply, currency and demand deposits, and MS_2 is the broader definition, which includes time deposits of commercial banks, average for December of the year indicated. The velocity here is income velocity (GNP/MS).

Complete the table below, and then answer the questions. (Monetary figures are given in billions of dollars.)

Year	MS_1	MS_2	GNP	V_{MS_1}	V_{MS_2}	Percent Annual Change MS_1	GNP
1950	$116	$153	$285	2.46	1.86	—	—
1956	137	189	419	3.06	2.22	1.5%	5.3%
1957	136	193	441	3.24	2.28	-.7	5.2
1958	141	207	447	3.17	2.16	3.7	1.4
1959	143	211	484	3.38	2.29	1.4	8.4
1960	144	217	504	3.50	2.32	.7	4.1
1961	149	229	520	3.49	2.27	3.4	3.2
1962	151	243	560	3.70	2.30	1.3	7.7
1963	157	259	591	3.76	2.28	3.9	5.5
1964	164	277	632	3.85	2.28	4.5	7.0
1965	171	301	685	4.01	2.28	4.3	8.3
1966	175	318	750	4.29	2.36	2.3	9.5
1967	187	350	794	4.25	2.27	6.9	5.9
1968	202	382	864	4.28	2.26	8.0	8.8
1969	209	392	930	4.45	2.37	3.4	7.6
1970	221	425	977	4.42	2.30	5.7	5.1
1971	235	473	1056	___	___	6.3	8.1
1972	256	526	1155	___	___	8.9	9.4
1973	271	571	1295	___	___	5.5	11.5
1974	284	614	1397	___	___	___	___
1975[a]				___	___	___	___

[a]It is suggested that you obtain later figures from the latest *Economic Report of the Council of Economic Advisers, Federal Reserve Bulletin,* or *Economic Indicators.*

Questions

1. Which concept of the supply of money generally gives a more stable value for velocity? _____

2. For a velocity of 3, what is the fraction of income held in money balances, on the average? _____

3. Do the figures seem to suggest a substantial change over the last 25 years in the desire to hold balances in the form of cash or demand deposits?

4. You will have noted from the first part that V_1 had substantial short-run fluctuations (part of the numerical stability in V_2 was due to rounding). Such shifts in velocity, of course, indicate a somewhat erratic relationship between money and income. If the data are examined, however, for a possible relationship between *rate of change* of the money supply and *rate of change* of GNP, something quite different might be noticed.

Make a test of the following hypotheses on the scatter diagram below, using observations 1957-1973:
  (a) The percentage change in GNP is a function of the percentage change in M_1.
  (b) The percentage change in GNP is a function of the percentage change in M_1 of the previous year.
Use x to record each observation in (a) and o for observations in (b). Fit a straight line, if it is feasible, to describe each relationship. Which hypothesis holds up in this test?

What is its approximate algebraic relationship?

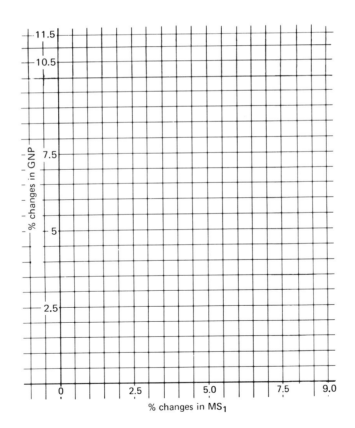

111

5.   What role might higher interest rates (about 5% to 7½% on time deposits instead of an earlier 3%) and price inflation in the 1966-1973 period have played in the higher V_{MS_1}?

6.   From the data above why might Friedman and other monetarists have shown a preference for MS_2 as a definition of the monetary supply?

PROBLEM 48

COMMERCIAL-BANK OPERATIONS

It is instructive for better understanding of the nature of commercial banking to look more closely at some of the principal assets and liabilities of commercial items, and at how they have changed over the post-World War II period. Below are compared the loans, investments, reserves, and demand and time deposits of member banks in 1947 with those in 1970 and 1973. Examine the figures and answer the questions. (Figures are given in billions of dollars.)

Totals for All Member Banks[a]	December, 1947	December, 1970	December, 1973
Loans			
Commercial	$16.9	$ 98.0	$134.4
Agricultural	1.0	6.5	10.2
Real estate	7.1	54.6	87.0
Individual	4.7	49.8	73.1
Other (mostly for purchases of securities and to other financial institutions)	2.9	45.6	86.9
Total loans	$32.6	$254.5	$391.4
Investments			
U.S. government securities	$57.9	$ 45.4	$ 60.6
State and local government bonds	4.2	55.7	72.0
Other	3.1	10.9	4.4
Total investments	$65.2	$112.0	$137.0
Reserves			
Deposits with Federal Reserve Bank	$18.0	$ 23.9	$ 27.8
Currency and coin	1.7	5.4	8.1
Total reserves	$19.7	$ 29.3	$ 35.9
Deposits, demand			
Private	$73.6	$147.5	$245.6
U.S. government	1.2	6.5	8.3
State and local	5.5	13.2	13.2
Total demand	$80.3	$167.2	$267.1
Deposits, time			
Private and other	$27.5	$161.0	$248.2
State and local	.7	18.4	33.3
Total time	$28.2	$179.4	$281.5
Equity capital accounts	$ 8.5	$ 34.1	$ 44.7

Source: Federal Reserve Bulletin.

Questions

1. We have seen that the reserves maintained by banks need be only a fraction of their deposits. However, banks recognize this possibly precarious reserve position by keeping most of their other assets in very liquid form. Loans other than mortgages are typically short term, and in the long-term bond account government securities are predominant.
    (a) Which was larger, total loans or total investments, in 1947? _____
In 1970? _____ In 1973? _____

(b) Show that the percentage increase in loans far exceeded the increase in investment over the period. Why is this change in asset mix probably consistent with profit maximization by the banks?

(c) Which category of loans, other than "other," has had the greatest rate of growth in the period? _____ Which category of investment? _____
(d) How might these shifts in bank portfolios be accounted for?

2. Member banks were required to keep reserves against time deposits of 5 percent in 1947; in 1973, the ratio was 5 percent for certain types of time deposits of large banks, and 3 percent for all other time deposits.
(a) Using 5 percent for 1947 and 3.5 percent as an approximation for 1973, estimate the amount of reserves that were held on account of time deposits in both years.
December, 1947 _____ December, 1973 _____
(b) By subtracting from total reserves, determine approximately the amount of reserves held on account of demand deposits. December, 1947 _____
December, 1973 _____
(c) Estimate the average reserve ratio for demand deposits. December, 1947 _____
December, 1973 _____
(d) Why would you expect excess reserves to be low during normal times?

3. What is the ratio of equity capital to deposit liabilities for commercial banks? If banks could loan money for 1% more than they pay in interest to depositors and in other expenses, what would this mean for profits?

PROBLEM 49

HIGH-POWERED MONEY

Several types of events create or destroy member-bank reserves. The major events are changes in Federal Reserve credit and changes in the public's need for cash. Some effects result also from changes in Treasury, foreign, and other nonmember bank deposits at the Fed, and from changes in monetary gold stock from Treasury purchases and sales of gold (with the gold stock essentially frozen, this has been an insignificant factor from 1968 to 1974).

Increases in the monetary gold stock supply reserves to the banking system (and decreases reduce reserves), whereas demands for cash by the public absorb reserves. Unlike the amount of Federal Reserve credit, these two factors are not under the control of the Fed, and officials spend considerable time trying to anticipate and, if need be, counteract undesired effects on bank reserves from these outside influences.

The term "Federal Reserve credit" means the acquisition of an asset by the Fed that either directly or indirectly supplies the member banks with equivalent reserve deposits. Open-market purchases are thus the primary sources of reserve bank credit; discounts (short-term loans) for member banks are a small fraction of the total. A rather interesting minor item of Federal Reserve credit is the "float," a graphic name for items in the process of collection and settlement among banks; the time lag in the process results in member-bank reserves receiving credit for items paid to them before those items are deducted from the reserves of the paying banks. A bad winter storm can delay the process even more and result in a temporary abnormal increase in the float and thus in member-bank reserves, but usually it is a stable and predictable item. Faster collection systems may reduce it gradually over time, although it would be expected to grow more or less in proportion to the value of total bank transactions.

It is instructive to set up what is called the "bank reserve equation," in which, much like a balance sheet, factors supplying reserve funds are balanced against factors absorbing reserve funds. Over a period of years, what factor has been largely responsible for the creation by the Fed of "high-powered money," the reserves of member banks on which the expansion of the money supply of the nation takes place?

Study the table on the next page and answer the accompanying questions. (Figures are given in billions of dollars and may not total exactly because of rounding and elimination of minor items.)

Member-Bank Reserves, Federal Reserve Bank Credit, and Related Items
(December, average daily)

	1945	1950	1960	1970	1973
Factor supplying reserves					
Federal Reserve credit					
U.S. government securities	$23.7	$20.3	$27.2	$61.7	$ 79.7
Discounts	.4	.1	.1	.3	1.3
Float	.7	1.1	1.7	3.6	3.4
Total	$24.7	$21.6	$29.1	$65.6	$ 84.4
Gold stock	20.0	22.9	18.0	11.1	11.6
Treasury currency outstanding					
(mostly coins)	4.3	4.6	5.4	7.1	8.7
Total	$49.1	$49.0	$52.4	$83.8	$104.7
Factors absorbing reserves					
Currency in circulation	$28.5	$27.8	$30.4[a]	$51.7[a]	$ 65.3[a]
Treasury cash holdings	2.3	1.3	.4	.4	.3
Nonmember bank, foreign, and other					
accounts at the Federal Reserve	2.4	2.6	2.3	1.7	3.0
Member-bank reserves	16.0	17.4	19.3[a]	29.3[a]	35.1[a]
Total	$49.2	$49.1	$52.4	$83.1	$103.7
Demand deposits of member banks,					
excluding U.S. government,					
December 31		$69.6		$168.0	

[a]From 1960, currency and coin in bank vaults has been subtracted from currency in circulation and included in member-bank reserves.
Source: Federal Reserve Bulletin.

Questions

1. From the figures given, fill out the following spaces to show changes in the major factors affecting bank reserves over the period:

	Change (+ or -), 1950-1970	Change (+ or -), 1970-1973
Factors supplying reserves		
Total Federal Reserve credit	_____	_____
Gold stock	_____	+.5
Treasury currency	+2.5	_____
Total	_____	_____
Factors absorbing reserves		
Currency in circulation	_____	_____
Member-bank reserves	_____	_____
Other accounts and equalizing		
adjustments	-1.1	+1.5
Total	_____	_____

2. The structure of the bank reserve equation clearly indicates that, assuming that no other changes take place, a rise in the amount of currency in circulation would have what effect on member-bank reserves? How do you explain that it was possible for both of them to rise together, 1950-1970?

3. *Ceteris paribus,* a decrease in the monetary gold stock would cause a decline in bank reserves and deposits. How did the Federal Reserve offset the effect of the gold outflow over this period?

4. What tool of monetary policy seems to have played a major role in determining the amount of reserves held by the member banks over this period? _____ If the aim of monetary policy over the period was to increase the amount of total money supply, was it successful?

5. Compare the ratio of reserves to demand deposits in 1945 and 1970. What tool of monetary policy might account for the difference in the two ratios?

FISCAL POLICY

PROBLEM 50

FISCAL DRAG AND THE FULL-EMPLOYMENT CRISIS

Before getting into the policy question, examine the following hypothetical situation:

1. Say that, for all levels of income, G will be $100 billion and net taxes (taxes minus transfer payments) will be $.25Y$. Plot G and T_n on the graph below, and answer the questions. Suppose that the full-employment level of GNP is $500 billion.

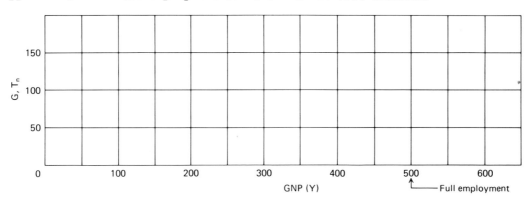

(a) The budget will be balanced at a GNP of _____.
(b) At GNP of $200 billion, the budget will show a (deficit/surplus) of _____.
(c) At full-employment GNP, the budget will show a (deficit/surplus) of _____.
(d) Suppose that, at full-employment GNP, I equals S and X equals M. Can this economy ever reach full employment with the fiscal policy depicted here?
(e) Show on the graph what two moves fiscal policy could make in this situation if full employment were the goal, and explain briefly.

118

2. Below is a graph of an aggregate-demand schedule for a hypothetical economy, showing an estimated full-employment level of 400 GNP.

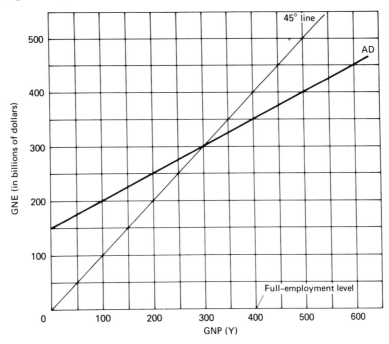

(a) What will be the *actual* GNP level in equilibrium? _____

(b) How big is the gap between actual and potential, or full-employment, GNP? *(Hint:* Measure along the horizontal axis.) _____

(c) How much of an increase in aggregate demand would be needed to move GNP from actual to full-employment GNP? *(Hint:* Measure along the vertical axis.) _____

(d) Explain in a few words why your answer to (c) is different from your answer to (b).

(e) What fiscal policy measures would be appropriate in this situation?

(f) Draw in the new AD curve, showing the elimination of the deflationary gap (assuming no change in slope).

3. Suppose that the government increases total spending by $10 billion per year and at the same time increases taxes so that it collects $10 billion more in tax revenues. Assume that $C = .60Y$ and $K = 2.5$

(a) The G spending increases aggregate demand by $10 billion and, via the multiplier, *increases* GNP by _____.

The arguments of the Council of Economic Advisers on behalf of the tax cut of 1964 made explicit use of the analysis of this and preceding chapters. The terms "fiscal drag" and "full-employment surplus" even seem to have originated with economists in the Kennedy administration, to describe the need for a less restrictive fiscal policy to reduce unemployment and stimulate economic growth.

The CEA's *Economic Report of the President* for 1964 described the concept of the full-employment surplus thus:

> The economic impact of a given budget program is best measured by its surplus or deficit at full-employment income levels. The surplus in the full-employment budget is too large when the Government demand contained in the budget, and private investment and consumption demands forthcoming from after-tax incomes, are insufficient to bring total output to the full-employment level. The actual budget will then show a smaller surplus or larger deficit than the full employment. . . .
>
> In a growing economy, periodic budget adjustments are required to maintain adequate expansion of total demand. The volume of tax revenues rises as incomes grow if tax rates remain unchanged. At present tax rates, the revenues that the Federal Government would collect at full employment increase by more than $6 billion a year. If program needs do not require expenditures to grow at the same rate, tax rates must be reduced, or a growing full-employment surplus will result, with increasingly restrictive effects on the economy.
>
> In the past this very process has been a major factor in slowing expansions and precipitating downturns. Thus, the consequences of excessive potential surpluses have been large actual deficits, unemployment, and inability to achieve steady growth.
>
> To avoid these consequences, an appropriate expansion-promoting fiscal program would call for tax and expenditure policies that prevent a constrictive rise in the full-employment surplus. The experience of the past 10 years has illustrated the tendency of full-employment surplus to build up to expansion-retarding levels as the economy grows. The tax reductions of 1964 will be a giant step to remove a burdensome fiscal restraint *before* the economy levels off or goes into a recession, and to provide a framework for continued vigorous growth.

Here are some figures with which the Council illustrated their point:

	1958	1959	1960	1961	1962	1963	1964
Full-employment (+ or -) surplus or deficit	+4.0	+6.5	+12.5	+8.0	+6.0	+8.0	+4.0
Actual surplus or deficit	-9.4	-1.1	+ 3.5	-4.5	-4.3	-2.8	-3.0
GNP, current prices	447	484	504	520	560	589	629
Potential GNP[a]	485	502	519	537	556	577	599
Actual GNP[a]	447	476	488	497	530	551	581

[a]1958 prices.

Questions

1. How do you account for the fact that the actual budget never had a surplus even close to the so-called "full-employment surplus" in any of the years given?

2. If fiscal policy is unchanging from year to year in its spending totals and in its tax structure, why might the "full-employment" surplus continue to grow larger? What is the proper remedy, according to the CEA?

3. In 1958, the Eisenhower administration drew up a budget that was expected to balance. What could have caused such a surprising deficit instead?

4. U.S. Federal Budget (in billions); Unemployment and Inflation Rates, 1969-1973

Year	Actual Budget Surplus	Change from Previous Year	Full-employment Surplus	Change from Previous Year	Unemployment Rate	CPI (1967 = 100)
1969	8.1	—	8.8	—	3.5	109.8
1970	-11.9	-20.0	4.0	- 4.8	4.9	116.3
1971	-22.1	-10.2	-2.1	- 6.1	5.9	121.3
1972	-15.9	+ 6.2	-7.7	- 5.6	5.6	125.3
1973	.6	+16.5	5.8	+13.5	4.9	133.1

(a) Judging from the figures above, how could the actual government deficits from 1970 to 1972 be explained?

(b) How is the actual deficit consistent with a full-employment surplus in 1970?

(c) What evidence is there of a significant shift in fiscal policy from 1972 to 1973? What problem was it evidently designed to meet?

(d) In 1974 the full-employment surplus approached $30 billion (although the actual budget was in slight deficit). What would you infer about the unemployment rate?

(e) In March 1975 a tax cut of $23 billion was voted with unemployment over 8 percent. An actual budget deficit approaching $75 billion was forecast. Explain the shift in policy。

PROBLEM 51

HOW A FISCAL SHOT IN THE ARM WORKED

Here is how the CEA in its *Economic Report* of 1964 described the way the gap of almost $30 billion between actual and potential GNP would be closed by the 1964 tax cut. (Personal income-tax rates were cut across the board from brackets of 18-91 percent to 14-70 percent. Corporate profit tax rates were cut from 30 to 22 percent of the first $25,000 and from 52 to 48 percent of the excess over $25,000.)

The process by which an $11.1 billion tax cut can add as much as $30 billion to total demand has been frequently described and needs only to be summarized briefly here.

If the new proposed personal income tax rates were in full effect today, disposable after-tax incomes of consumers would be approximately $8.8 billion higher than they are, at present levels of pretax incomes. In addition, if the lower corporate tax rates were now in effect, after-tax profits would be about $2.3 billion higher. Based on past dividend practice, one can assume that corporate dividends received by individuals (after deducting personal income taxes on such dividends) would then be more than $1 billion higher, giving a total increment of consumer after-tax incomes—at present levels of production—of about $10 billion.

Since consumer spending on current output has remained close to 93 percent of disposable income in each of the past dozen years, one can safely project that consumer spending would rise by about 93 percent of the rise in disposable incomes, or by over $9 billion. . . .

But this is far from the end of the matter. The higher production of consumer goods to meet this extra spending would mean extra employment, higher payrolls, higher profits, and higher farm and professional and service incomes. This added purchasing power would generate still further increases in spending and incomes in an endless, but rapidly diminishing, chain. The initial rise of $9 billion, plus this extra consumption spending and extra output of consumer goods would add over $18 billion to our annual GNP—not just once, but year-in and year-out, since this is a permanent, not a one-shot, tax cut. We can summarize this continuing process by saying that a "multiplier" of approximately 2 has been applied to the direct increment of consumption spending.

But that is not the end of the matter either. For the higher volume of sales, the higher productivity associated with fuller use of existing capacity, and the lower tax rates on corporate profits also provided by the tax bill, would increase after-tax profits, and especially the rate of expected after-tax profit on investment in new facilities. Adding to this the financial incentives embodied in last year's tax changes, which are yet to have their full effect, one can expect a substantial induced rise in business plant and equipment spending, and a rise in the rate of inventory investment. Further, higher consumer incomes will stimulate extra residential construction; and the higher revenues that state and local governments will receive under existing tax rates will prompt a rise in their investments in schools, roads, and urban facilities. The exact amount of each of these increases is hard to estimate with precision. But it is reasonable to estimate their sum as in the range of $5 to $7 billion. This extra spending would also be subject to a multiplier of 2 as incomes rose and consumer spending increased. Thus there would be a further expansion of $10 to $14 billion in GNP to add to the $18 billion or so from the consumption factor alone. The total addition to GNP would match rather closely the estimated $30 billion gap.

The tax cut worked very much as predicted. Later, inflationary difficulties came from the second shot in the arm, an increase of over $28 billion from 1965 to 1968 in federal defense expenditures mostly reflecting the Vietnam escalation.

Questions

1. Write the equation for the CEA's marginal propensity to consume out of disposable income. _____ .

2. The CEA assumes that incremental withdrawals are about what fraction of incremental incomes? _____

3. How could a reduction of corporate income tax rates result in an increase of disposable personal income?

4. Total increase in disposable income predicted from the tax cut is _____ . Total increase in consumer spending predicted initially from the tax cut is _____ . When multiplied it would add how much to the GNP? _____

5. For what reason does the CEA also predict a rise in investment to occur?

6. Why does the Council expect state and local governments to increase their spending?

7. Total anticipated increases from 5 and 6 above, when multiplied, are predicted to add how much to GNP? _____

8. Total rise in GNP predicted from the tax cut is _____ .

9. Illustrate on the diagram the expected effect of the tax cut of 1964 on the full-employment surplus. Draw an approximate T-schedule for 1963 and one for 1964, and label them. (Federal *G* rose by $1 billion in that year, from $64 billion to $65 billion.)

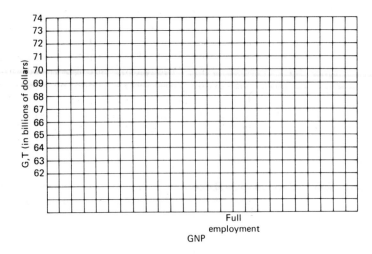

124

PROBLEM 52

THAT ELUSIVE TRADE-OFF BETWEEN
UNEMPLOYMENT AND INFLATION

Page 1 of *The New York Times* on January, 1969, carried the following story:

> President-elect Richard M. Nixon will take office at a time when the nation's unemployment is at its lowest point in years.
> The Labor Department reported today that the rate of unemployment in December had held at the 15-year low of 3.3% of the labor force achieved in November. . . . The rate for the year as a whole was 3.6%. . . .
> The reduction in unemployment last year, however, was small—from 3.8% in 1967 to 3.6% in 1968. A counterpart of this small "bonus" in employment was the biggest rise in prices in 17 years.
> Many economists, including some who will advise the new administration, think that this "trade off" has become a losing game—that more inflation, reflecting booming spending and production, is now producing relatively few additional jobs in the American economy.

(a) Does this quotation suggest an L-shaped curve, a Phillips curve, or both?
   _____

(b) If the advisers referred to prevail, what fiscal and monetary policy measures might be expected, in general? _____

Use the raw material below to plot a Phillips or L-shaped or whatever-shaped curve. Plot the percentage price changes and the corresponding employment rate for each year on the graph, indicating the year beside each point you plot. Fit a curve by eye as best you can.

Year	(1) GNP Price Deflator[a] 1958 = 100	(2) Percentage Change in Prices from Preceding Year	(3) Unemployment Rate, Percent of Labor Force[a]	(4) Employment Rate, 100 − (3)
1955	90.9	—	4.4%	95.6
1956	94.0	3.4%	4.2	95.8
1957	97.5	3.7	4.3	95.7
1958	100.0	2.6	6.8	93.2
1959	101.7	1.6	5.5	94.5
1960	103.3	1.7	5.5	94.5
1961	104.6	1.3	6.7	93.3
1962	105.8	1.1	5.5	94.5
1963	107.2	1.3	5.7	94.3
1964	108.9	1.6	5.2	94.8
1965	110.9	1.8	4.5	95.5
1966	113.9	2.1	3.8	96.2
1967	117.6	2.7	3.8	96.2
1968	122.3	4.3	3.6	96.4
1969	128.2	4.7	3.5	96.5
1970	135.2	5.5	4.9	95.1
1971	141.6	4.9	5.9	94.1
1972	146.1	3.2	5.6	94.1
1973	154.3 (est.)	5.6	4.9	95.1
1974	170.1	10.2	5.6	94.4

[a]*Economic Report of the President*, 1975.

125

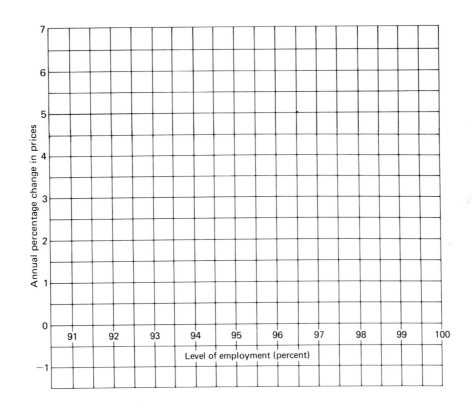

(a) Is the prediction of the Phillips curve borne out that prices will gradually fall if unemployment becomes sufficiently large? _____ Do the data fully test the prediction as stated in this question? _____ Why would it be difficult to test the prediction fully at the present time?

(b) Is the further prediction of the Phillips curve borne out that the price level will rise more rapidly as unemployment is reduced, and that the rate of increase in the price level will decline as unemployment increases?

(c) What evidence do you see that possibly the Phillips curve has shifted upward and to the left since 1967?

PROBLEM 53

DOES THE UNITED STATES NEED
WAGE-PRICE GUIDEPOSTS?

As President Ford took office in the summer of 1974, he received close to consensus forecasts of almost 10 percent inflation and modest recession with an unemployment rise to over 6 percent. His initial policy proposal of a gradually reduced rate of monetary growth and a cut in federal expenditures was directed toward controlling inflation and apparently implied the acceptance of recession. The option of an "incomes policy" was attractive if it allowed more stimulative fiscal or monetary policies without as much inflationary impact.

Such an incomes policy could take several forms of varying vigor:

(a) The *Council on Price and Wage Stability,* which might restrain price setting and wage settlements by publicly pointing out significant "abuses." This was set up by Ford and could evolve into (b):

(b) *Explicit wage-price guideposts,* which are the subject of this case and which prevailed between 1962 and 1966.

(c) *Mandatory price and wage controls,* a largely self-administering form of which was used by the Nixon administration between August, 1971, and the spring of 1974. After some success in 1971 and 1972, the controls proved relatively ineffective against the commodity price inflation of 1973-1974. Ford categorically rejected the idea of using them.

The case experience with the wage-price guideposts is worth examining, because an "incomes policy" seems likely to remain a policy option that will be considered in the future, and because the guidelines are likely to be standards for policies ranging from occasional "jawboning" to mandatory controls.

The Guideposts Announced

The ideas behind the wage-price guideposts—namely, cost-push inflation and widespread discretionary power over wages and prices exercised by unions and oligopolistic firms—were articulated before 1962. Official government pronouncements had called for responsible behavior by labor and business leaders, and the implication that wage rises in line with general productivity advances could be consistent with a generally stable price level had been widely discussed. In the last economic report of the Eisenhower administration, the Council of Economic Advisers (Raymond Saulnier was chairman) had concluded, "The only way to assure that, for the economy as a whole, maximum employment and maximum production also mean maximum purchasing power is to keep wage improvements generally within the range of productivity advance."

In 1962, the Council, with Walter Heller as chairman, made the wage-price guideposts explicit.* The chapter devoted to "Price Behavior in a Free and Growing Economy" concluded with six pages on "Guideposts for Noninflationary Wage and Price Behavior." A fundamental question was posed: How is the public to judge whether a particular wage-price decision is in the national interest? The guides that follow were the council's answer (it was recognized that difficulties remained):

The general guide for noninflationary wage behavior is that the rate of increase in wage rates (including fringe benefits) in each industry be equal to the trend rate of over-all productivity increase. General acceptance of this guide would maintain stability of labor cost per unit of output for the economy as a whole—though not of course for individual industries.

The general guide for noninflationary price behavior calls for price reduction if the industry's rate of productivity increase exceeds the over-all rate—for this would mean declining unit labor costs; it calls for an appropriate increase in price if the opposite

---

Economic Report of the President, 1963.

127

relationship prevails; and it calls for stable prices if the two rates of productivity increase are equal.

These are advanced as general guideposts. To reconcile them with objectives of equity and efficiency, specific modifications must be made to adapt them to the circumstances of particular industries. If all of these modifications are made, each in the specific circumstances to which it applies, they are consistent with stability of the general price level. Public judgments about the effects on the price level of particular wage or price decisions should take into account the modifications as well as the general guides. The most important modifications are the following:

(1) Wage rate increases would exceed the general guide rate in an industry which would otherwise be unable to attract sufficient labor; or in which wage rates are exceptionally low compared with the range of wages earned elsewhere by similar labor, because the bargaining position of workers has been weak in particular local labor markets.

(2) Wage rate increases would fall short of the general guide rate in an industry which could not provide jobs for its entire labor force even in times of generally full employment; or in which wage rates are exceptionally high compared with the range of wages earned elsewhere by similar labor, because the bargaining position of workers has been especially strong.

(3) Prices would rise more rapidly, or fall more slowly, than indicated by the general guide rate in an industry in which the level of profits was insufficient to attract the capital required to finance a needed expansion in capacity; or in which costs other than labor costs had risen.

(4) Prices would rise more slowly, or fall more rapidly, than indicated by the general guide in an industry in which the relation of productive capacity to full employment demand shows the desirability of an outflow of the capital from the industry; or in which costs other than labor costs have fallen; or in which excessive market power has resulted in rates of profit substantially higher than those earned elsewhere on investments of comparable risk.*

Kennedy and Steel

The major concern of the Council's 1963 *Report* was with tax reduction and reform designed to stimulate growth and full employment (unemployment was 5.6 percent in 1962). Wage and price guideposts were reviewed in this context:

The principal threat to the continuation of price stability in 1962 occurred in April when a general increase in steel prices was announced by a number of major producers. This increase followed the agreement in March on a wage contract generally regarded as noninflationary. Had this increase stood, it would have caused and invited other price increases throughout the economy; it would have led organized labor to adopt a new militancy in its wage demands; and it would have seriously weakened the forces working toward the restoration of our international competitive position. Fortunately, the price increase was rescinded after the President expressed the country's concern over the serious threat to price stability and our balance of payments.**

The *Report* did not mention that to achieve these results the Kennedy administration had used its influence to achieve a more modest wage settlement than those in the past. Nor did it mention the confrontation between President Kennedy and the steel executives, in which the President not only appealed to their sense of public responsibility but threatened government investigation and possible legal proceedings under the antitrust laws. The decisive event in the conflict was the willingness of a few producers such as Inland, Kaiser, and Armco to hold the line.

---

*Ibid., p. 189.
**Economic Report of the President, 1963.

The main policy recommendations of President Johnson's first *Economic Report* (1964) were early tax reduction (unemployment in 1963 was 5.5 percent) and the War on Poverty. A wage guidepost of 3.2 percent was stated implicitly: "The appropriate standard for annual percentage increases in total employee compensation per hour (not just in straight-time hourly rates) is the annual increase in *national trend* output per man hour" (p. 118). A table (p. 114) showed trend productivity of 3.2 percent, the average of the five preceding years. In January, 1965, the national trend rate was again recognized as 3.2 percent in the first report issued under Gardner Ackley's chairmanship. Tax reductions amounting to about $8 billion had been passed in 1964; proposed tax reforms had been rejected.

By January, 1966, the economic situation had changed substantially. In his message to Congress (the first section of each *Economic Report of the President),* Lyndon Johnson recognized that 1.5 percent of GNP and 200,000 men were involved with Vietnam, and that largely through a surge in agricultural and food prices "the wholesale price index which had been at 1958 levels for six years jumped two percent."

Significantly, in retrospect, although a vigorous economy was expected in 1966 (unemployment had dropped from 5.0 percent to 4.1 percent in the preceding 12 months), no tax increases to pay for Vietnam were called for.

For the maintenance of cost-price stability, the president recommended:

> The basic precondition for price stability is a fiscal-monetary policy that deters total demand for goods and services from outrunning potential supply. But history proclaims that something more is needed: a sense of responsibility to the public interest by labor and business in setting wages and prices.
>
> The vigorous economy we foresee in 1966 will tempt labor unions to demand wage increases that would raise costs, and businesses to raise prices when profit margins are already fully adequate. Labor must remember that growing employment and productivity are the foundation of higher wages, and business that an expanding economy is the basic source of profit gains. These foundations must not be jeopardized.
>
> The attached Report of the Council of Economic Advisers contains a thorough discussion of its guideposts for noninflationary wage and price behavior. To maintain price stability in the expanding economy of 1966, it is vitally important that labor and industry follow these guideposts.*

The Council of Economic Advisers recognized some new problems in the 1961-1965 expansion. Unit labor costs in the private economy (compensation per man-hour divided by output per man-hour) had been remarkably stable since 1960, reflecting wage rises within the 3.2 percent suggested by the wage guidepost. However, in certain areas (e.g., retail trade) the workers had been relatively low-paid, and in construction, where unions faced weak employers and bargaining, wages increases in 1965 were well above the suggested rates.

The price increases of 1965 in part reflected these higher wage costs. Prices also rose substantially in industries affected by increased demand, as in agriculture and particularly in basic metal industries. Profit margins increased in wide areas of the economy.

The national trend productivity measure now showed a 3.6-percent rise in productivity, which would require an increase in the wage guidepost; but this represented in part the rise in efficiency that occurs with operations closer to capacity, rather than a sustainable long-run rate.

To meet these problems the Council suggested the following in January, 1966:

1. Special measures that might be taken to meet problems of rising prices in particular areas, such as encouraging technological advance, making it easier to get entry of skilled workers in the construction industry, and supplying more facilities and personnel for medical services.

2. The maintenance of the 3.2-percent wage guidepost, since with the continued expansion the 3.6-percent average rise in productivity for the last five years was no longer

---

Economic Report of the President, 1966.

representative of long-run growth possibilities. No recession years were now included in the average.

3. Emphasis on the price guidepost in these words:

The guideposts must continue to aim at complete stability of average domestic prices. While individual prices will rise from time to time, others must fall if upward pressure on the general price level is to be avoided. . . . Every management with some market power must ask itself: Is a price increase justified by increase in costs? . . . And those companies with exceptionally favorable productivity gains must consider whether this is the time to seek to keep the gains in the form of still higher profits, or whether to share them with consumers through lower prices.*

Inflation Knocks Out the Guideposts

By the end of 1966, the specific wage guidepost of 3.2 percent was dead. The Consumer Price Index had risen by 3.3 percent. In its 1967 *Report,* the CEA noted that "in the areas in which the guideposts were expected to apply—among strongly organized groups of workers and in firms which have appreciable discretion with regard to their prices—the guideposts were reasonably well observed until at least mid-1966." The two conspicuous failures of the wage guideposts came in the New York subway strike and the airlines strike, both settled, after government intervention, at far above the guidepost percentage. The primary source of price increases was recognized to be in areas where the guideposts were not applicable, but the Council emphasized that there had been a failure to reduce prices where called for by the guideposts.

The basic problem in 1967 for the Council was whether to propose a new guideline, one that would allow for the cost of living. They decided not to because wage rises including the productivity trend plus the rise in the cost of living would necessarily perpetuate price rises. Their own prediction, a reasonably accurate one, was for a slower rate of expansion in 1967, with less excess demand pressure. They reviewed cost-push (as distinct from demand-pull) inflation and the original 1962 statement on the wage and price guideposts. The 1967 *Report* recommended a 6-percent income-tax surcharge and favorably commented on the easier credit conditions after the "credit crunch" of mid-1966, which actually had decreased the money supply.

Economists Test Effects of Guideposts

The contribution of the guideposts was reviewed by Congress in January, 1968, in hearings before the Joint Economic Committee on "The Wage-Price Issue—The Need for Guideposts." Econometric studies by G. L. Perry and G. Fromm were presented. Their findings were consistent with the hypothesis that the wage guidepost made a significant difference from 1962 to 1966 in the rate of change in hourly earnings of manufacturing and, through the influences on unit labor costs, on prices.

The fundamental approach was the following: Percy set up the hypothesis that the percentage change in hourly earnings was a function of (1) the percentage change in the Consumer Price Index of the preceding period, (2) the inverse of the percentage unemployment rate, (3) the profit rate of the preceding period, and (4) the change in profit rate (profits divided by equity). Fromm used similar techniques and variables.

Essentially, it was found that the equation that accurately predicted the change in wages from 1947 to 1960 substantially overpredicted the rise from 1962 to 1966. Percy supplemented this finding by showing that wages in such "visible" industries as the automobile industry advanced by relatively less in the 1960s than wages in the 1950s in such "invisible" industries as the textile industry. The wage bargains in visible industries were much more subject to publicity than those in invisible industries.

The testimony emphasized the basic importance of monetary and fiscal policy and conceded that the effectiveness of guideposts could be significant only in a noninflationary economy because wages and prices in the industries most affected by the guideposts could scarcely be

---

*Ibid.

held down when other prices and wages were rising rapidly. It also recognized that other factors such as increased import competition could have helped the relative performance in the 1960s.

Nixon's Economic Advisers and the Guideposts

The following paragraph from the CEA's 1971 *Report* sums up the Administration's opinion of the guidepost approach at that time.

There is now a great deal of experience to indicate that the superficially attractive route of voluntary controls is unlikely to lead to a solution. By "voluntary controls" is meant a system in which the Government, or a quasi-independent board selected by the Government, specifies comprehensive standards of wage-price policy to be observed voluntarily by labor and business, without any similarly comprehensive means of enforcement by Government. The basic deficiency in this approach is that it counts on a large number of people to acquiesce in conduct that they find contrary not only to their own interests but also to their view of fairness, propriety, and efficiency. The great initial attraction of the idea, that it makes the public think something effective is being done, is also one of its adverse consequences because it distracts attention from the real nature of the problem.*

Questions

1. In the Congressional hearings, economist John Sheahan stated, "In a highly flexible, perfectly competitive economy there would be no place for guideposts." Why?

2. The guideposts seemed to have a helpful effect when prices were almost stable, but were relatively ineffective after prices rose. Explain.

3. Why do you think the CEA was hesitant to revise the wage guidepost to include an allowance for rises in the cost-of-living index?

---

*Economic Report of the President, 1971, p. 79.

4. What measures might the government take to "unleash and strengthen those forces of the free market that hold prices down"?

5. In the fall of 1974, Professor James Tobin of Yale was one of the strongest proponents of an "incomes" policy that would allow monetary and fiscal policy to keep unemployment from rising and to achieve a 4-percent annual growth in production. He suggested a wage guidepost of 8 or 9 percent. Assuming that three-fourths of the growth was in productivity, what rate of average price increase is implied?

6. Might the guideposts be useful under present circumstances? What principles from them might be useful?

7. The following exercise should help you see why the general guidelines are noninflationary and also imply a stable distribution of income.

In 1973, the Fuddy Dud Corporation was producing under the conditions indicated below. At the time, early 1974, that the union negotiated a wage increase (as shown), labor productivity (output per man-hour) rose by 5 percent through some plant changes. Fill in the blanks below.

Year	Employees	Hourly Wage	Hourly Pay-roll	Output of Duds per Man-hour	Unit Labor Cost	Total Hourly Output	Market Price per Dud	Total Hourly Revenue
1973	100	$3.00	_____	10	$.30	_____	$1	_____
1974	100	$3.12	_____	10.5	_____	_____	$1	_____

(a) Compare the increase in the hourly payroll with the increase in total hourly revenue. Assuming that all output is sold and that there are no other changes, does this company seem more or less profitable than before? _____

(b) Should this wage increase justify a price increase? _____

(c) If this were a competitive industry, what does theory predict would happen to the price of this product, *ceteris paribus*?

(d) Suppose that output per man-hour remained unchanged, instead of rising. Unit labor cost would become _____. Total hourly revenue will be _____. What effect will this have on profits if the price is not increased?

INTERNATIONAL ECONOMICS; MONEY AND TRADE

PROBLEM 54

WHAT PRICE FOR GOLD?

In September, 1974, almost half of the world's gold stock was tied up in monetary reserves with a nominal value of $42.22 per ounce, set by the United States's definition of the gold equivalent of the dollar. This was a nominal figure, because reserves were generally not available for purchase or transfer. At the same time, the free-market price for gold in London was fluctuating around a price of $160 an ounce. Legislation was passed by the U.S. Congress legalizing the ownership of gold by U.S. citizens on December 31, 1974 (or earlier if approved by President Ford). One Washington brokerage house predicted that legalization of private ownership would produce "a stampede" driving the price shortly up to $400 an ounce. A study by the First National City Bank of New York saw a realistic range between $118 and $135 an ounce, considering the demand by buyers who wished gold as an inflation hedge. (The U.S. price level was rising by over 10 percent a year and that in most developed countries by somewhat more.) Banks, commodity exchanges, and department and jewelry stores were preparing selling services to satisfy demands from 1/5 ounce to the standard bar of 400 ounces.

Clearly the worth of gold was a much more complicated question than in the period from 1933 to 1967, when the United States stood ready to buy or sell gold at $35 an ounce for official foreigners. The $35 had been an effective floor with free-market prices occasionally rising to $40 when rumors suggested that devaluation was likely. (Black-market prices could be significantly higher in countries with a hoarding tradition and bans against private possession.)

To cast some light on the question of worth, some estimates of gold supply and demand will be examined. Professor Triffin gave the following figures for stocks on hand at the end of 1957 (the estimates for gold that disappeared into hoards and industrial uses are admittedly conjectural). Changes since then have been estimated from the sources listed.

Gold Stock and Uses (millions of ounces)

	1957	Change 1957-1970	1970	Change 1970-1973	1973
Total gold stock	1,720	610[a]	2,330[a]	135	2,475
Gold in monetary reserves	1,110	110	1,210	-30	1,180
Disappeared into:					
Arts and industry	390	170	560	120	680
Hoards and speculative holdings	220	340	560	45	605

[a]Includes an estimated 120 million ounces of Russian shipments but excludes 60 million ounces of possible Russian production during this period. In addition Russia may have stocks of 150 million ounces.

Sources: Robert Triffin, *Gold and the Dollar Crisis* (New Haven: Yale University Press, 1960); annual editions of the *Mineral Yearbook; Federal Reserve Bulletin,* various issues.

The Supply Situation

The sources of newly mined gold can be divided into three categories: South Africa (65-70 percent), the USSR (10-15 percent), and the world outside South Africa and the USSR (over 15 percent).

For virtually all countries in the last category, production has been declining. Some production has been subsidized, as in the Philippines, but even there production increases have been slight. In the United States, about one-third of the production is a by-product of copper mining, where the ore contains only .004 of recoverable gold per ton of ore ($.14 worth). Total U.S. production decreased from 4.8 to 1.4 million troy ounces annually between 1940 and 1973.

It seems probable to many observers that the Russians incurred costs of over $35 per ounce for much of their output, because their need for foreign exchange for strategic purchases from the West was great. The situation in South Africa has been quite different. That country has more than doubled its production since 1953, and in 1967 it produced more than the whole world did in 1953. It actually reduced its working cost per ounce of gold from an estimated $26.21 in the 1953-1957 period to $20.69 in 1967, by increasing gold recovery per ton and making other technological advances.

As world prices rose in the 1970s, South African gold mining costs rose somewhat, partly because of government requirements that low-grade resources be used to extend the life of the mines.

World production in 1972 in millions of troy ounces was: South Africa, 29.2; USSR, 6.7; Canada, 2.1; United States, 1.4; all others, 6.8, for a total of 46.2.

The Demand Situation

The demand for gold can be broken down into four categories: for monetary purposes, for industry and the arts, for hoarding, and for speculation.

Before 1967, monetary demands absorbed any residual of new gold into internationally acceptable reserves. (Although some countries occasionally mint gold coins that can be sold at a 10- to 20-percent premium to hoarders, no country really uses them as money or permits domestic convertibility.)

Only about one-fourth of the industrial demand has been for technical uses for such purposes as electrical connections and heat transfer. The rest has been for dentistry and the arts. Some of this demand, such as for solid gold ashtrays or bracelets, may reflect the same motives as hoarding. By 1973 fabrication approximated 45 million ounces, a total close to total production of newly mined gold.

Both in Europe, where sharp wartime inflations have taken place, and in Asia, where by tradition gold has been valued as a store of wealth, the hoarding demand has been strong. The blurred line between hoarding and speculation is that the hoarder seeks to maintain the value of his wealth in real terms, whereas the speculator seeks rapid and substantial profits. Speculative demand is essentially a function of the strength of expectations that the real price of gold will rise. The risk to the speculator was low as long as monetary demand could be counted on to take excess supplies off the market at $35 an ounce and he could purchase at close to $35 an ounce. His main cost was the opportunity cost of giving up a return on income-earning assets, but a change in the monetary price to $70 or even $50 could compensate him for this many times over.

The Two-Tier System and Subsequent Developments

Between September, 1967, and March, 1968, the gold reserves of the world dropped from a little less than $43 billion to a little over $40 billion, with U.S. reserves taking over half the drop (from 12.1 to 10.7 billion). These billions had been fed into the private markets to maintain a private price of close to $35 in the face of heavy speculation that the official gold price would be raised.

In March the leading financial nations set up the two-tier system, in which the United States agreed to maintain the $35 for official reserves only and all of the nations involved agreed neither to sell nor to buy gold from the private market, including any newly mined gold.

134

Private market prices during the rest of 1968 fluctuated around $40, substantially lower than the crisis peak of almost $45. South Africa withheld most or all of its supplies from the private market and added to its own reserves as it sought an agreement that at least the IMF would step in to support the price at $35, which it in effect obtained despite U.S. opposition. The major supplies for the private markets thus came from stocks of speculators who now risked losses and had become pessimistic about a new higher price in the future. The South African strategy seemed to be to nurse the premium on gold in the private market and to hope to use the two-price system and to enhance its average price by taking off the surplus at $35.

The Devaluations in 1971 and 1973

In 1971, although industrial demand rose by less than the long-run average of 9 percent a year, more than the total production of 41 million ounces went into industrial and hoarding use. South Africa sold gold reserves. The free-market price crept up and by January, 1972, was over $44. It had edged downward temporarily when the Administration committed the United States to raising its official price from $35 to $38 an ounce. In 1973, gold prices increased rapidly both before and after the United States floated the dollar and then raised the official price of gold to $42.22. The London price ranged from $64 to $127 an ounce in 1973.

The Outlook in 1974

As indicated in the supply-and-demand analysis above, newly mined gold could probably take care of all industrial and arts needs at costs apparently far below $100 an ounce. The key uncertainty was the future role of gold in the monetary system. Under the system of flexible rates in 1974, little use was being made of accumulated gold reserves with their nominal value of $42.22 an ounce. European countries had generally been pushing for higher valuations of gold reserves against the opposition of the United States, which wished to minimize the role of gold in international transactions and favored the use of SDRs and exchange rates sufficiently flexible to minimize the need for large reserve holdings.

Questions

1. As long as the United States was, in effect, committed to maintaining the price of all gold at $35, what was the elasticity of demand for gold at that price?

2. What would the increase in world monetary reserves have been if the nominal price of $42.22 per ounce had been changed to a fixed and effective price of $150?

3. At the time you are reading the case:
   (a) For what price can you buy gold?

(b) What valuation is being used for official gold holdings?

(c) Would it have been a good investment if an American had purchased gold as soon as it became legal?

4. What consequence might the demonetization of gold in the near future have on the gold price (remember that official reserves have been 20 to 25 times as great as the supply of newly mined gold)?

5. How is the nonmonetary supply-and-demand situation for gold fundamentally different from that of silver (see case, "Did the Silver Make the Quarter Valuable?")?

6. The median annual rate of cost-of-living rise (currency depreciation) was 3.2 percent from 1957 to 1967 in a 44-nation sample compiled by the First National City Bank of New York. Most leading industrial nations did better. The United States had the least rise among the group—1.7 percent—a record that was tarnished by the 1967-1971 price rise of over 4 percent a year. Brazil had the greatest inflation, at 31.6 percent per year. In contrast, from mid-1973 to mid-1974 the cost-of-living rise was over 10 percent in the United States and was substantially greater in most countries. How might this development influence the hoarding demand?

PROBLEM 55

"I DON'T GIVE A (EXPLETIVE DELETED) ABOUT THE LIRA"

The title quote is President Nixon's reply to an observation about possible currency speculation in a taped conversation with H. R. Haldeman (June 23, 1972). The President found international monetary issues "too complicated" and uninteresting: "Only George Schultz [the economist and Secretary of the Treasury] and people like that think it's great. . . . There's no votes in it, Bob." Nonetheless his administration led the world's switch from the Bretton Woods system of fixed exchange rates within a narrow band to floating or flexible rates.

In the late 1960s, international monetary crises occurred with increasing frequency as fixed rates got out of line with the long-run realities of changing national productivities or rates of domestic inflation. For example, in November, 1968, when the mark was valued at $.25 and the franc at $.20255, the Germans resisted an upward revaluation of the undervalued mark because of fears it would damage export business, and the French under DeGaulle said *"Non"* to the devaluation of an overvalued franc largely because of national pride.

On August 15, 1971, President Nixon formally suspended the right of foreign governments and central banks to acquire gold from the U.S. Treasury at $35 an ounce and imposed a 10-percent temporary surcharge on most dutiable imports. The first move had the effect of floating the dollar by putting other nations on notice that the United States was no longer prepared to support exchange rates fixed at the then existing levels. The import surcharge was designed to improve the U.S. current-accounts balance, which for the first time in 34 years had shown deficits for 4 months in a row, and to lend bargaining power to obtain later trade and/or monetary concessions.

The Administration's action followed a decade in which the American dollar was felt by many economists to be somewhat overvalued because of the greatly developed production capacity of Europe and Japan. The war in Vietnam, because of its requirements for foreign exchange and because of the inflation it set off in the United States, had put the balance of payments more seriously in deficit. In 1971, lower interest rates in the United States set off a massive out-flow of short-term capital, which was escalated by rumors of currency devaluation. In May, West Germany and Holland floated the mark and the guilder, and Switzerland revalued its currency upward. In the first quarter of 1971 alone, the U.S. deficit in official reserve transactions was $5.5 billion.

Chapter 40 evaluates the implications of these events for the future of the world monetary system; now we emphasize the impact on exchange rates. Other countries, particularly France, urged the United States to devalue by increasing the official, although nominal, price of gold. After months of denials and maybes, the United States in December, 1971, agreed to raise its nominal price of gold to $38 an ounce (subject to later congressional action) and to eliminate the 10-percent surcharge. Agreement was reached on the new fixed parities in the table below with provision for fluctuations of 2¼ percent (instead of the old 1 percent) on either side.

These adjustments in parities were not sufficient to prevent continued massive deficits in the U.S. balance of payments, and in February, 1973, the United States decided to let the dollar float for the indefinite future. Its devaluation of the dollar in terms of gold to $42.22 per ounce was only symbolic, because the United States no longer permitted the conversion of gold held by official foreigners into dollars.

The following table shows the changes in exchange rates from August, 1971 to 1974, for selected countries.

Exchange Rates for Selected Countries from 1971 to 1974

		Rate (Fixed Parity) 8/12/71	Fixed Parity 12/20/71	High-Low Between 3/73 and 2/74[b]	Rate 8/7/74
Canada	dollar	.9878[a]	.9958[a]	1.0016-.9918	1.0237
United Kingdom	pound	2.4200 (2.40)	2.6057	2.5762-2.2240	2.3730
France	franc	.1818 (.18)	.1955	.2466-.1991	.2125
Italy	lira	.001613 (.0016)	.00172	.00177-.00153	.00154
Switzerland	franc	.2496 (2448)	.2604	.3543-.2973	.3365
West Germany	mark	.2966[a]	.3103	.4282-.3553	.3862
Japan	yen	.0028 (.00278)	.00325	.00382-.00336	.00351
Brazil	cruzeiro	.1900[a]	.1810[a]	c	.1475
Mexico	peso	.0801 (.08)	.0800	.0800-.0800	.0801
Sweden	krona	.1938 (.1933)	.2078	.2473-.2078	.2290

[a]No fixed parity.
[b]Monthly averages; most highs were in July, 1973, and lows in January, 1974.
[c]Averages not available in *Federal Reserve Bulletin*.

Questions

1. By about how much did most foreign currencies deviate from their parities on August 12, 1971? Compare this with their fluctuations from March, 1973, through February, 1974.

2. In addition to the lira, what currencies depreciated in terms of the dollar between 1971 and 1974? What does this depreciation probably signify concerning rates of domestic inflation within these countries?

3. What was the apparent policy of Mexico toward floating the peso?

4. What was the indicated lira price of the mark in August, 1971, and in August, 1974?

5. By what percentage did the franc price of the mark appreciate between the parities of November, 1968, and August, 1974?

6. The Volkswagen manufacturing company, highly dependent on American sales, ran into difficulties in 1973 and 1974. What reason for this is suggested by the exchange rates above?

PROBLEM 56

TWO REQUESTS FOR PROTECTION FROM IMPORTS

In 1951, the year of Mr. Torbert's testimony given below, the steel industry seemed reasonably satisfied with the essentially free-trade conditions under which it operated, both for raw materials and for most of its products. It produced over 45 percent of the world's steel, 97 million tons of a total world output of 208 million tons, and was a substantial net exporter of steel, both as steel products and as a component of transportation equipment and heavy industry.

The trade policy that Mr. Torbert was protesting, and in which the steel industry later sought modification, was the gradual lowering of tariffs through the arrangement of reciprocal concessions with foreign nations. Beginning in 1934, the United States has gradually moved away from strong protectionism under liberalizing legislation that at every renewal time was heavily challenged by industries that felt particularly threatened by it. As described below, this policy received at least a temporary setback in 1971 with the 10-percent ad valorem surcharge on most dutiable imports. For the steel industry, the second example, "voluntary" import quotas somewhat stemmed the tide of imports after 1968.

The Vitrified China Industry

The following are excerpts from the statement by E. L. Torbert on January 26, 1951, before the House Ways and Means Committee in Hearing on H. R. 1612, an Act to Extend the Trade Agreements Act of 1934.

Mr. Chairman, my name is E. S. Torbert. I am vice president of the Onondaga Pottery Company, Syracuse, New York, and chairman of the foreign trade committee of the Vitrified China Association, which association represents two-thirds of the vitrified china production in the United States.

I am here to continue our protest against the Reciprocal Trade Treaty Act and its effect upon the vitrified china industry in particular and the handcraft industries in general.

The vitrified china industry in the United States needs adequate tariff protection if it is to continue to exist in a condition of healthy activity. To survive and thrive the vitrified china industry needs tariff protection for the very ordinary and simple reason that china can be produced abroad, transported to this country, and sold here at a price below that at which American potteries can produce and sell their product.

The problem is, in essence, purely a wages problem. The American employer cannot afford to pay American wages and sell in competition with the distressingly low wages paid in so many foreign countries. Currently the wages paid to American pottery workers in the vitrified china industry are about 4 to 4½ times wages paid English pottery workers, 6 times the rate paid German pottery workers, and 12 times the rate paid Japanese pottery workers. . . .

The economic effects of accepting without duty foreign products which come into this country merely and solely because of the low wages paid the laborers who produce them are in many respects virtually the same as would be the effects of importing those foreign laborers and having them work for the low wages received in the foreign country.

We contend that, in a country like the United States which years ago restricted immigration because it felt that it was no longer in need of an increased labor force, and in which a fairly large amount of unemployment is becoming normal, a country which is already much more highly mechanized than any other country in the world, no efficient and well-managed industry should be allowed to disappear or even be crippled merely because it does not admit of extreme mechanization and because of that fact—with the necessarily accompanying high percentage that wages are of its total costs (about 2/3 of total costs were labor costs)—is unable to compete unaided with the products of low-wage foreign competitors.

We contend, further, that it is virtually a breach of faith for the United State Government to throw such an industry to the dogs—or indeed in any way to ignore it—merely to help some of our over-developed mechanized industries to throw their products on foreign markets.

But something more than jobs for Americans, something going even deeper than protection of American workers from low-cost labor of other countries, is involved in the tariff on pottery.

Our country needs the pottery industry. It needs it not only for employment and wages but also because few other industries attract a similar group of skilled workers and artisans. Few others impart to their workers an equal pride in creating beauty as well as a product of lasting and enriching satisfaction completely unknown to the assembly line automation whose whole energies are bent, for instance, to bolting fenders. . . .

The only ancient craft which exists today as a great industry and yet remains a craft is deserving of fair and full consideration in the broad picture of our current hopes for peace, prosperity, and human advancement.

The Steel Industry

The annual review of the industry for 1967, *Charting Steel's Progress,* prepared by the American Iron and Steel Institute, New York, noted the following major challenges: (1) rising employment and other costs; (2) intensified competition from other materials and from an unrestricted flood of low-cost foreign steel. It cited the industry's responses as a vigorous program aimed at improvement of technology and the development of new and better products. Even though its rate of return on capital investment (measured by total assets minus current liabilities) was a relatively low 4.9 percent, its capital expenditures were over $2 billion (over $1 billion net). Because 1964 output and employment in 1964 had been on a plateau, the 1967 decline brought it back to approximately 1964 levels.

The Institute reported on world production and imports as follows:

Foreign countries as a whole produced more steel during 1967 than ever before. The world total was 546 million net tons of raw steel, up 5 percent from 1966. (The figure was 654 million tons in 1970.)

Simultaneously foreign steel penetrated the U.S.A. more deeply than at any time. Nearly 11.5 million net tons of imported steel mill products cost the American steel industry over 12 percent of its home market. The incoming tonnage was 6.5 percent higher than in 1966. As a result American producers, who experienced declines in steel output and shipments for the year, redoubled their efforts to have Congress limit imports by a system of quotas to approximately 10 percent of U.S. domestic consumption. They pointed out that while incoming foreign steel rose to an all-time high in tonnage and dollar value, this country's exports of steel declined 2.3 percent during 1967, worsening the U.S. position in world steel trade and aggravating the balance of payments deficit in steel.

Around the world steelmaking capacity continued to exceed production, with the result that foreign producers increasingly invaded the markets of other producers, the greatest competitive battle being waged in the United States.

Over 60 countries poured raw steel last year and nearly all of them shipped steel mill products to the United States, now the world's largest importer of steel even though it still remains the largest steelmaking nation.

The U.S. made 23 percent of the world total, producing 127.2 million tons of raw steel, a 5.1 percent decline from 1966. (The figure was 131.5 million tons in 1970.)

The United States was on the receiving end of 11,454,502 net tons of foreign-made steel, with an all-time dollar valuation of nearly $1.3 billion. For the preceding year the figures were: 10,753,000 net tons, valued at $1.2 billion.

Meanwhile exports of steel from the U.S.A. declined slightly to 1,685,000 tons, from 1,724,000 in the preceding year. The 1967 exports were valued at nearly $415 million against $420 million in 1966.

The deficit in this country's world steel trade amounted to an estimated $1.1 billion, having negative impact on the balance of payments. The $1.1 billion is arrived at by adding freight charges, insurance and allowances for government-financed exports to the $877 million excess of the valuation of steel imports over the valuation of steel exports.

The effect of the steel industry request for a 10% (of U.S. consumption) import quota was to induce Japan and the E.E.C. each to set quotas on exports to the U.S. of 5,750,000 tons for 1969 with a provision of a 5% annual increase thereafter. 1970 imports of 13.4 million tons were 13.8% of apparent U.S. consumption. Increased U.S. exports helped hold the U.S. trade deficit in steel to about one billion dollars.

Questions

1. Do these requests for protection indicate that the United States was at a comparative disadvantage in producing china? _____ In producing steel? _____

2. How apt was Mr. Torbert's comparison of china imports with immigration in its economic effects?

3. Is there any similarity between protecting hand and semimechanized industries and their workers from import competition and protecting them from technological innovation?

4. What alternative goal to economic efficiency does Mr. Torbert suggest?

5. What argument is presented by the American Iron and Steel Institute for quota protection for steel?

6. What preliminary hypotheses can you offer to explain the U.S. switch from the largest exporter to the largest importer of steel? Are they consistent with the substantial improvement in exports and reduction in imports of steel that followed the depreciation of the dollar from 1971 to 1973?

7. How can the U.S. maintain increases in total exports sufficient at least to equal total imports when in such basic commodities as steel and passenger automobiles it has become a net importer?

PROBLEM 57

BREAKING THROUGH THE PRODUCTION-POSSIBILITIES WITH TRADE

In each of the cases below, assume a two-nation, two-product model in which no trade is taking place. The two nations, Austerity and Bacchanalia, henceforth referred to as A and B, make their production and consumption choices between products X and Y. Assume that both nations have identical patterns of tastes and preferences and that they are such that, when the products are equal in price, equal quantities will be consumed. In each case, after trade commences, assume that the prices are equal and that the consumption of X and the consumption of Y will be equal in each country. Perfect competition is assumed in product markets.

In each of the graphs below, you are given the production-possibilities frontier and the price and quantity produced and consumed before trade (indicated by the dots). The before-trade relative prices (P_X/P_Y) are given by the slope of the production-possibilities curve. Show the amount that will be produced and consumed by each after trade when $P_X = P_Y$. Note that when trade does take place, each nation in its consumption will have broken through its production-possibilities frontier. For questions on absolute advantage you should assume the same quantities of factors in each country.

Complete the table below on the before-trade conditions as you work with each case.

Before-trade conditions	1	2 (and 2a)	3	4	5
Opportunity cost of X (in terms of Y) in country A[a]	_____	_____	_____	_____	25/36
Opportunity cost of X (in terms of Y) in country B[a]	_____	_____	_____	_____	36/25
P_X/P_Y in country A	_____	_____	_____	_____	_____
P_X/P_Y in country B	_____	_____	_____	_____	_____

[a]At existing production levels.

Case 1

(a) A has an absolute advantage in the production of _____. B has an absolute advantage in the production of _____. Therefore, A has a comparative advantage in the production of _____ and is at a comparative disadvantage in the production of _____.

(b) With the opening of trade, A will produce _____ of product _____; B will product _____ of product _____. With P_X/P_Y, A will export _____ units of product _____ and import _____ units of product _____.

(c) Both countries will have gained because A can now consume _____ more units of _____ and B _____ more units of _____, each while maintaining its consumption of the other product. P_X/P_Y is greater than before in country _____ and less than before in country _____.

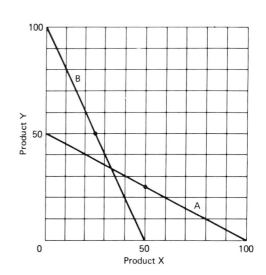

Cases 2 and 2a

(a) In case 2, there (is/is not) an absolute advantage for either; there (is/is not) a comparative advantage for either.

(b) In case 2a, country A has a(n) _____ advantage in both products. It has no _____ advantage because opportunity costs are the _____, as reflected in relative prices of the products, which are _____. There (will/will not) be trade.

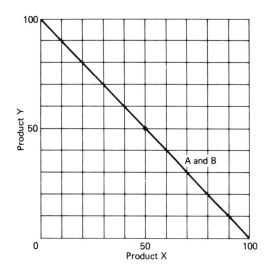
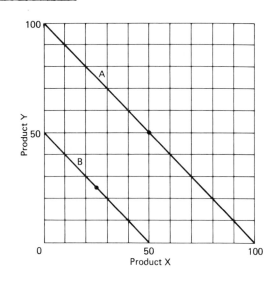

Case 3

Again, in this case there is apparently no absolute advantage or comparative advantage.

(a) This case differs from case 2, where opportunity costs were constant, since when either country expands its production of X or Y units it encounters _____ opportunity costs for that product in terms of the other. If trade is opened up, it therefore will pay one country, say A, to _____ in the output of X, and the other country, say B, to _____ in the output of Y.

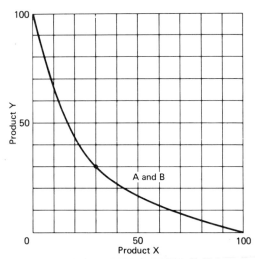

(b) With such specialization, A will establish a comparative advantage in X and B in Y, and with P_X/P_Y, A will export _____ of X in exchange for _____ of Y. Both countries will be at consumption levels beyond their _____ and will have gained by trade _____ units of each commodity.

144

Case 4

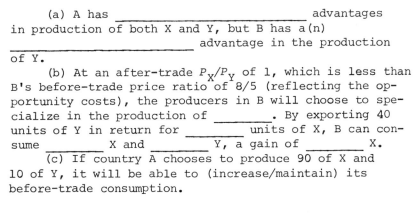

(a) A has _____ advantages in production of both X and Y, but B has a(n) _____ advantage in the production of Y.

(b) At an after-trade P_X/P_Y of 1, which is less than B's before-trade price ratio of 8/5 (reflecting the opportunity costs), the producers in B will choose to specialize in the production of _____. By exporting 40 units of Y in return for _____ units of X, B can consume _____ X and _____ Y, a gain of _____ X.

(c) If country A chooses to produce 90 of X and 10 of Y, it will be able to (increase/maintain) its before-trade consumption.

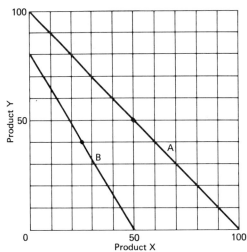

Note: You may be concerned about why the gains of trade go entirely to B. This reflects the assumption both of perfect competition and of the particular demand conditions that allowed P_Y to continue to equal P_X. For A to gain, it would be necessary that the after-trade price ratio be more favorable for product X, in which it has the comparative advantage. The complexities of this problem of price determination belong in a more advanced course in international trade, but you should recognize this much: If country A can keep the price ratio of X:Y just below 8:5, B's producers will still find it profitable to offer Y in trade because trading for X will be cheaper than producing it. One way of accomplishing this would be for A to place a tariff on product Y of almost 60 percent (37½/62½). B could then get only .62½X instead of 1X for each unit of Y, and most of the gains of trade would go to A.

Case 5

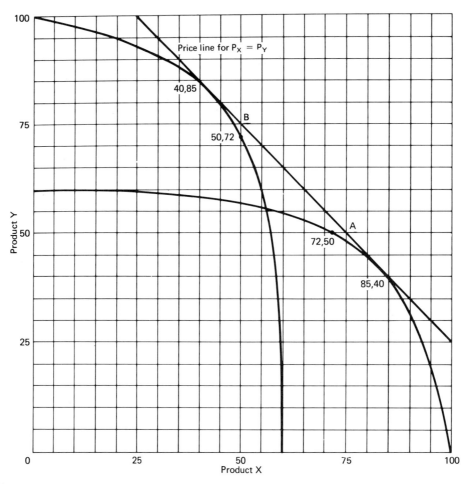

Price line for $P_X = P_Y$

40,85

B

50,72

A

72,50

85,40

Product Y

Product X

(a) In this case, the opportunity costs vary with the production level. In each country, the opportunity cost of each product becomes _____, the more that is produced. For any given production level, the opportunity costs in A are less for product _____, and in B for product _____. Thus, the comparative advantage in A is for product _____ and in B for product _____.

(b) Even with trade complete, specialization will not occur because the opportunity costs become very _____ as all resources are devoted to the output of one good. Cases 1, 2, and 4 can be termed as cases of constant costs, case 3 as one of decreasing costs, and this case as one of _____ costs.

(c) Trade can take place at P_X/P_Y because in country A at before-trade consumption levels the opportunity cost of producing more X is _____ than 1Y, and in country B the opportunity cost of producing more Y is _____ than 1X. Thus, A will _____ its production of X from 72 to 85, where the opportunity cost is _____Y, and B will increase its production of Y from 72 to 85, where the opportunity cost is _____ X.

(d) Total production of X for both countries together is now _____, instead of the before-trade _____. Total production of Y is likewise _____, instead of the before-trade _____.

(e) To achieve the equal consumption of both commodities called for by the demand assumptions, A will export _____ in return for _____. This new consumption point can be found on the graph on the price line with the slope of 1, which is _____ to the production-possibilities frontiers at the points of after-trade _____.

146

75 76 77 6 5 4 3 2 1